Hollywood Values

By

Steven C. Scheer

*For Marcia Yudkin,
my favorite mentor!
Stvn C. Scheer
December 2006*

ISBN: 0-7596-7114-1

This book is printed on acid free paper.

1stBooks – rev. 0 /0 /02

For Nita, with affection

"Movies aren't boring. Life is boring. Movies are real."

—Something Short of Paradise

Table of Contents

Preface

Have you ever felt that while you and your friends watched the same movie, you didn't really *see* the same movie? Have you ever wondered why people see so many different things in movies? A few years ago I had an opportunity to hear Michael Medved in person. He is the author of *Hollywood vs. America* (1992). What he said about *Titanic* (1997) shocked me. He said the movie was "corrupt" because it shows that all an old woman remembers late in her life is the fact that when she was young "she got laid in the back seat of a car." At that time I had not seen the movie yet, but some instinct told me that there must be more to this story than that. Sure enough, when I did get a chance to see the movie, I saw something entirely different. What the old woman remembers is, of course, making love to the young man she fell in love with on that fated voyage, a young man who loved her so much that he, for all intents and purposes, gave up his life that she might live. Since "greater love has no man," I didn't think there was anything "corrupt" about this, but it is this sort of negative reaction to Hollywood that has prompted me to write *Hollywood Values*. I intend it as a foil, if you will, to a lot of fashionable Hollywood bashing that passes for criticism these days.

If you like movies, this book is for you. My larger purpose in writing it has been the conviction that (like all works of literature) movies are arguments that present us with stories which exemplify the never-ending struggle between good and evil and which are thus, even if at times indirectly, concerned with our most sacred values. Hollywood has, of course, produced so many movies that the ones covered in this book can barely represent the tip of the proverbial iceberg. In spite of this necessary limitation (and the fact that I have also limited myself to movies produced in the last 20 years), I feel that the four categories under which I carefully examine a wide variety of movies do give us an adequate sampling of the good things that can come out of Hollywood. The categories are basic: going to school, falling in love, fighting for justice, and making a difference. I treat four movies under each of these categories, each with a different and thought-provoking perspective on a given theme in question. I should also mention that what you will find in this book is not a series of movie reviews, but fully considered readings aided and abetted by my many years of experience as a teacher of literature and as a literary critic.

At the same time, this is not a dry, academic work, but a work devoted to a heartfelt appreciation of movies and to as accurate a representation of what they are about as is humanly possible.

I grant you that not all movies are good, but I will also assert that the good ones *are* very good and are thus worthy of our undivided attention. I read the ones I treat in this book carefully, keeping my eyes and ears scrupulously focused on what we see and hear at all times, for the devil (no pun intended) is always in the details. It is for this reason that I meticulously go over what happens (and what is said) in each movie while interpreting it. In order to see the meaning or the significance of a given movie, we must pay attention to all the parts that make up the whole (which—if all goes well— is usually greater than the sum of its parts). If we are willing to really see and hear, we can be richly rewarded. But we should keep an open mind. Giving in to what I call the "rejective imagination" won't do.

Take "language," for example. Some people are still bothered by so-called adult language used in many movies. They don't seem to see that just as it is possible for a good person to use "adult language" and still be good, it is also possible for a bad (or even an evil) person never to utter a "bad" word. It is not words, per se, that are good or bad. It is something else entirely. We should look beyond the surface. We shouldn't judge a book by its cover, or a movie by its language. Although in this book (with the exception of a rare and unavoidable quotation here and there) I use no "objectionable" language, I do feel that to object to words while overlooking meanings (as Studs Terkel once remarked) is not worthy of our humanity.

We can't learn from movies if we don't enjoy them. And we can't enjoy them if we keep objecting to what is not part of what really matters. Movies can tell us a great deal about our world. They can teach us valuable lessons about life and even about our own selves. All we need to do is keep an open mind and not let the head reject prematurely what our hearts are willing to embrace. *Hollywood Values* is about good movies. I hope that reading about them will inspire you to revisit them and to enjoy them in renewed ways. This would be my greatest reward for having written this book.

Acknowledgements

Although I have a large personal library (about 5,000 volumes) and have bought many movies in VHS format (with a few DVDs of late as well), I found two Web sites on the Internet that have been invaluable sources of information. In fact, I was able to do most of my research for this book on the Internet. I would like to single out two particular sites that are nothing short of amazing. The first is the Internet Movie Database (http://www.imdb.com/). It is a veritable encyclopedia of movies made the world over. And it's all for free. They do accept donations (if you are a customer of Amazon.com the process is painless and well worth the effort), and they do deserve whatever you can spare. The second is a Web site called Simply Scripts (http://www.simplyscripts.com/). This site has literally hundreds of screenplays available for reading and study. I wish to express a debt of gratitude for the people who have created and who are maintaining these sites. They have certainly made writing this book a lot easier than it would otherwise have been. Any factual errors that remain are, of course, my own.

Introduction

1. Why I Wrote This Book

"How did you become an English major?" my students used to ask me. The answer would usually take me back to my native Hungary, all the way back to the year 1948 (or perhaps 1949), to when I was either 7 going on 8 or 8 going on 9. I am no longer sure which, perhaps the latter. In any case, one day my grandmother gave me money to go to the movies. There was a feature-length Russian cartoon showing in my neighborhood theater in Budapest called, I am sure of this, "The Tale of the Firebird." It so happens, though, that the day I went to see this movie, they changed to the Laurence Olivier production of *Hamlet* (1948). Not being one to allow minor disappointments to interfere with my plans, I bought a ticket and was promptly seated to see something I had not the faintest idea about.

When the show began, I immediately noticed the foreign language. At this point I am not even sure whether or not I knew that the language in question was English (I think I did), but I still remember that the language sounded as if the people who spoke it had cotton in their mouths. Actually, after all these years it is difficult for me to remember myself as a person who did not understand English, but I know that that was the case once.

Now please keep in mind that in this particular case I was either 8 or 9. And also that the subtitles to *Hamlet*, being a Shakespeare play, were not in any way or shape or form abbreviated. Yep, I still remember the struggle with which I kept bravely up with reading four or five or even six lines on the bottom of the screen at a time. Somehow or other I managed as best as I could. And I must say that I pretty much understood the whole story. Well, I understood its plot. And, upon reflection on my way home afterwards, I thought it was a pretty good movie.

So I told my friends about it. I still remember telling them the whole story. How Hamlet's father's ghost appears to him and tells him that his stepfather had actually killed him, etc. Being the age I was then, I probably skipped most of the "stuff" about Ophelia, though I still remember lingering with ample attention on the duel between Hamlet and Laertes (and, yes, I was fully aware of the treachery). In any case, a few days after my telling my friends all about *Hamlet* someone warned me not to come down to the playground where we used to hang out. The reason?

Lots of my friends had wanted to beat me up for recommending such a boring movie to them.

Yes, I date my becoming an English major to that particular event in my life. Even though it wasn't until some years later, by the time I was just about 16, that the Hungarian Revolution of 1956 broke out. And it wasn't until at the end of that year that my mother and I left Hungary, with untold thousands upon thousands, never to return (except for visits much later). And it wasn't until 1959, when I came to the United States at the age of 18, that I began to learn English. Let me add here, though, that the first book I ever bought myself (today I have a private library of over 5,000 books) was Shakespeare's *Hamlet.* I regret to say that the particular edition (a Washington Square Press Edition for 35 cents) is no longer in my possession.

Needless to say, my love of literature as well as my love of movies became a reality in my life way before I was truly conscious of the fact. I took it for granted. But the real lesson of my *Hamlet* story (and, I am happy to report, my little friends did not beat me up, after all) is that if beauty is in the eye of the beholder, boredom may well be in the heart and mind and soul of (well) the boree. I did not find *Hamlet* boring. My peers did. I guess what I am driving at is, in some sense, rather obvious. We look at the same thing, but we don't see the same thing. We listen to the same words, but we don't hear the same words. We may watch the same movie, but we don't see the same movie.

This brings me, rather suddenly, up to the 1980's. We are now in Evansville, Indiana. And I have just seen, repeatedly (each time with greater and greater pleasure), Milos Forman's *Amadeus* (1984). I was so enamored of this movie that I couldn't help myself. Once more I just had to tell my friends all about it. At one point the neighbor of my girlfriend, tiring of hearing my accolades for Mozart, said, point blank, that Wolfgang Amadeus was a (gulp) "idiot savant." I still feel the shock when I remember those words. Is this what my girlfriend's neighbor saw in *Amadeus*? Is this how he interpreted Mozart's childlike naiveté which, because of its accompanying lack of a sense of diplomacy, elicited such concealed hatred from the odiously mediocre Salieri that the latter took on the role of Satan in order to destroy God's creation because he resented the fact that God gave the gift of beautiful music to such a vulgar little man?

The moral of *this* story is the same, in a way, as the moral of the *Hamlet* story. It is a moral that's repeated endlessly by countless millions of people in all walks of life. Again, we may look at the same thing, but we don't see the same thing. We may listen to the same words, but we don't hear the same words. We may watch the same movie, but we don't see the same movie. The question is, must it be this way? Must it be this way all or at least most of the time? Can't we get closer together to what a given movie may actually be "saying" and/or "doing"? As a teacher of literature for more than a quarter of a century, I think the answer is "yes." And I won't use the customary word ("education"), though, of course, it isn't entirely irrelevant. What I want to hint at, rather, is that love is the root of all beauty and that where beauty is truth and goodness may not be far behind. This is not to say that *we* are the sole sources of beauty and truth and goodness. What we do, when we do what we do well, is *respond* to the same even in movies by attending to the heart of the matter, by not succumbing to the rule of unexamined prejudices, by not jumping to conclusions. As I say elsewhere, in an essay called "The Art of Reading," to read well, we must to a point ignore ourselves and give ourselves over to the text, or to the sights and sounds of the screen. Before rejecting, we should really pay attention, so that the beauty, the truth, and the goodness that may really be there, outside of us, in the movie itself, may have a chance at revealing themselves to us in us, coming to fruition in our responses to the sights and sounds of the screen.

It is with some such "attitude" as this that I took it upon myself to write this book, *Hollywood Values*. I know that many of us love movies and many of us see good things in them. But I hope that walking through together a selected number of them here we may come to appreciate what's in them even better. It is not true that analyzing a work of art destroys it. It may be that under certain circumstances not to say something is the right thing, for even a single word may spoil the mood, and it may also be true that under certain other circumstances silence is golden, but when it comes to talking about movies, about what we like—nay, love about them, we may actually be giving renewed life to our perceptions and understanding. Sometimes we don't really know what we mean until we say it first (as W.H. Auden, I believe, once said).

2. Obstacles to Understanding and Enjoyment

Hollywood values. A contradiction in terms? There are, of course, many who may not value the values Hollywood proffers. Especially since the country had been overtaken by a conservative mood that doesn't seem to be vulnerable to change. It has been fashionable to bash Hollywood for decades now, and not just from the same quarters. Most conservatives don't think Hollywood is traditional and/or conventional enough in its values. Most liberals like Hollywood just fine, but (along with most radicals) they think that independent films are better than the tired same old same old coming out of Hollywood these days.

Who among these various constituencies has gotten it right? If beauty is in the eye of the beholder, maybe values reside in some such place, too. I would suggest the heart. Or the heart and mind and soul of the beholder. One person's poison may well be another's medicine. Like it or not, we now live in a pluralistic or multicultural society. And I am using this last term in its broadest descriptive sense. Your next-door neighbor may be conservative or liberal. He or she may be for or against abortion and/or capital punishment. May or may not believe in God. May or may not believe in organized religion. May be a theist (or a deist even) or a pantheist or an atheist. A Jew or a Christian. A Muslim or a Buddhist. Or just an agnostic.

Traditionalists think that the world is going to hell in a hand basket. Radicals think that we are drowning in the tired rhetoric of received opinion. Fundamentalists think that only the Bible is true and everything else is just "man's ideas" (or the devil's). Most other people think that the fundamentalists are deranged. Lots of people pride themselves on being open-minded, but when push comes to shove, they shove. And this applies to conservatives and liberals alike. The extreme right is foaming at the mouth at everything modern and/or (gulp) postmodern, while the extreme left has for a while now been completely bereft of all semblance of common sense. The biblically correct despise the biblically incorrect while the politically correct are just as intolerant of the politically incorrect, and everyone is more or less wary of all views they disapprove of—and what do they *not* disapprove of among them?

It seems that everybody thinks that everybody else is suspect unless, of course, they belong to the same like-minded group or toe the same party line. In the meantime (in my humble opinion) everybody is both right and wrong (to a point). The trouble is that few people can rise to the occasion of compassionate understanding, the compassionate understanding of *other* people and *other* points of view. Habitual ways of thinking confine us to seeing no more than what habitual ways of thinking have already processed and accepted as "true." Although it is easy to show that habitual ways of thinking are actually the greatest enemies to critical thinking, habitual ways of thinking do possess tremendous staying power. Yet such unthinking thinking is no thinking at all. It is no more than the mere parroting of other people's thoughts, thoughts which may well be chock full of errors hidden in the folds of unquestioning acceptance. The blind leading the blind, if you will.

Hollywood is part and parcel of this ragtag bag of tricks. Or is it? And are we all, for that matter? I think that what I have been saying so far is true to a point, but I don't think that it is absolutely true. Nor do I think that things are as hopeless as they seem to be. I am pessimistic when I see the human capacity to be locked into various and sundry unseemly worldviews created by various and sundry ill-conceived ideologies, but I am also optimistic when I perceive the equally powerful human capacity to break out of the bondage various and sundry ways of thinking impose upon us from time to time.

The trouble is that once we have learned to see things a certain way, we develop a resistance to changing those ways of seeing things. We come to trust what we already know and we tend to defend it even in the light of overwhelming evidence to the contrary. Freud once observed that our convictions are mixtures between the true and the false and that in defending them we automatically defend the false with the true. The American humorist Josh Billings once quipped that it is "better to know nothing than to know what ain't so." Since it is impossible to know nothing (for by the time this question comes up we always already know or seem to think we know something), is it not possible that at least some of what we think we know may not be so?

To be closed-minded means that you think you know all there is to know already. That you are an old dog who doesn't *need* any new tricks. To be open-minded means that you are still capable of learning something new, though this new knowledge is, of course, itself vulnerable to be a mix between the true and the false. Which of these is better? I don't think it takes much imagination to see that it is better to be open-minded than to be closed-minded. The latter may well be the living dead, for all we know.

In any case, those who are absolutely certain that they are absolutely right about absolutely everything already will never learn anything new. Or they'll automatically and instantaneously reject whatever new thought will come at them. The open-minded are, on the other hand, young dogs, ever after the scent of new tricks. They run the risk of being misled, but they are alive and well. And if they become flexible-minded to boot, they will always have the capacity to learn from their own mistakes, from the errors of their own ways. The closed-minded have stopped growing. The open- and/or flexible-minded never grow old (at least in spirit).

The word "liberal" has been a dirty word for decades now. This may be due to a certain confusion, in part, as well as to a certain change in how liberals themselves go about plying their trade. Looking at definitions in good dictionaries I have come up with the following: A liberal is a person who is favorable to progress or reform, as in political and religious affairs. A liberal is a person who is likely to advocate individual freedom of action and expression. A liberal is also likely to favor representational forms of government as opposed to aristocracies or monarchies. A liberal person is also likely to be (or will strive to be) free of prejudice and bigotry. Such a person also tends to be tolerant. According to one definition, a liberal person is the person who is not likely to be bound by traditional or conventional ideas or values. According to yet another definition, a liberal person is generous and is characterized by a willingness to give freely and abundantly to those who are less fortunate. Furthermore, a liberal person is not likely to be strict or rigorous in his or her judgments and is not prone to be literal-minded about rules and regulations. These are, of course, the characteristics of the classic view of liberalism, not of its politically correct tendencies that may be responsible for its bad name in certain circles these days.

A conservative person, on the other hand, is bent on preserving existing conditions and institutions, interested in keeping to the status quo (not necessarily a bad thing). He or she is not willing to change, is likely to mistrust change, in fact, on the grounds that if something isn't broke, it should not be fixed (not in itself a bad idea). A conservative person is not disposed to automatically admire whatever is novel or showy. A conservative person favors whatever he or she thinks has stood the test of time. Nowadays conservatives are also opposed to too much government, particularly of the centralized sort. Here's where to my mind at least they overlap with liberalism in its classical sense. What conservatives and liberals have in common is a shared dislike and mistrust of certain forms of totalitarianism. Totalitarianism is given to a centralized form of government that does not tolerate parties of different ideologies and tends to exercise a dictatorial control over all aspects of life. There is no freedom of action and/or expression in a totalitarian state.

Totalitarian states may be fueled by religion or by certain political ideologies. Christendom in the Middle Ages, for example, was absolutist and thus totalitarian. It not only blocked scientific discoveries, but was also willing and able to punish those who dared to contradict the teachings of the Church. "Creation science" comes close to this sort of totalitarian attitude in our day. It is easy to see that various forms of fascism (including Nazism) and communism have been totalitarian in their basic outlook. And it should also be easy to see that in a totalitarian world "Hollywood" would have to toe the party line and produce nothing but propaganda, centrally approved movies with firmly pre-established themes and values, themes and values approved of by the government, whether religious or political.

This is clearly not the case in America. We live in a democratic society. Our republic may not be perfect, but it may be as good as it gets (no pun intended on the fine movie by that name). The lack of consensus on many issues is here to stay. "We were as Danes in Denmark all day long," says Wallace Stevens in "Auroras of Autumn," but we are so no longer. Today we are more likely to be as Danes in Italy or as Italians in Russia or as Hungarians in Denmark. Feeling like strangers in our own homes, as it were. This is not to say that our various religious and/or political institutions do not rightly disapprove of certain things, but it does seem to me at least that these days we are living in an atmosphere of apparently irreconcilable mutual mistrust. Freedom of expression is alive but not always well. Attempts at censorship under one guise or another keep rearing their ugly heads. The movies have, in fact, been censored for a number of decades in the name of decency and/or respectability. The results have not always been good. The sacrifice of artistic integrity may at times undermine thematic significance as well. The only movies that can't offend anyone are movies that don't show and/or say anything of value to anyone at all. I doubt that the majority of people would want nothing but movies that endlessly repeat pre-approved formulas of beauty and goodness and truth. It's not that we would be drowning in boredom, it's that we would become intellectual zombies, the living dead, devoid of hearts and minds and souls.

3. The Business of Art

According to a classical formula (formulated in Horace's "Art of Poetry"), the business of art is to teach and to delight. Of course, when the moral of a story reads too much like a lesson, the art is diminished and frequently dismissed on the grounds that it is too didactic. Thus, there can be too much teaching in art, though whether there can be such a thing as too much delight remains a moot question. For those who suffer from anhedonia any delight is too much delight, but even on more reasonable grounds the argument could be made that when a work of art has nothing but "delight" going for it, it runs a risk of being merely frivolous.

I personally have always been uneasy with people who demand that movies do nothing beyond entertaining them. I have never found a movie that did nothing but entertain—well, entertaining. The pleasure comes, among other things, from understanding, understanding the insights into life that a movie can deliver perhaps in spite of itself. It is not that moviemakers intend to preach (though that can happen, too); it is just that what they show and tell will contain useful information, knowledge, and (preferably) even wisdom. The famous quip about "messages" and "Western Union" notwithstanding, almost all movies have something to say, something of value, perhaps even something invaluable.

But the word "business" plays another role in the title of this section. Movies are works of art, but they are also in the business of making money. Whether they teach more than they delight or delight more than they teach is a moot question when it comes to whether or not they are expected to make money. Anticipation of box office success or failure plays a prominent role in how movies are financed and made. In an ideal world artistic talent would be enough to get a movie made and, if made well, it would automatically do well with the public, too.

Actually, the public has a great deal of power, more than most people realize. Since anticipation of box office success or failure is determined by second-guessing of what the public might or might not like, the vagaries of public taste play a significant role in determining what kinds of movies get made. If producers could know for sure, only moneymaking movies would be made. As it is, mistakes occur at all levels. Some movies flop, some that should flop make it big. This may actually benefit the public at large. Many tastes go into the making of movies and it takes many tastes to appreciate them all. Not everyone likes every movie. Whether some people have better taste than others is a moot question. According to an old Latin saying there is no point in quarreling over tastes anyway. Some like it hot (no pun intended on the fine movie by that title) while others like it cold (whatever that may mean).

Because the movie-making industry is apt to keep a cold eye on profits, screenwriters and directors are less likely to have the unhampered artistic freedom and the complete creative control they might wish for. Which, again, is not necessarily a bad thing. Though freedom is an essential part of artistic creation, movie-making is a result of team work where changes are bound to be made so that by the time the public gets to see a movie the whole may or may not be greater than the sum of its parts.

In *Hollywood Values* my primary concern is with the final product. I shall concentrate on themes—that is, on meaning and significance. Camera work and other technicalities do not interest me any more than fonts interest me when I read a novel. What I shall also concentrate on is the pleasure of the sounds and images that confront us when we watch a movie. As far as I am concerned, movies are part of "literature" (a kind of combination between plays and novels, though some come close to poetry in their lyricism). Movies can create and/or expose myths in all senses of the word. They can be for or against certain beliefs and ideologies. They can be critical or even subversive of received opinion. They can challenge and move us. They can appeal to our basest or to our most noble instincts. They can show us why people can be terrible or wonderful. They can make us laugh or cry. They can make us feel. And think. And know. They can make us see.

None of this can happen, of course, if we approach movies with unseemly prejudices. Good readers are receptive, not "rejective." There is altogether too much rejection going on these days, and not just rejection of movies. If we are to enjoy as well as to understand (and these two are intricately linked), we must approach movies with open and flexible minds. With open and flexible hearts, too. According to old wisdom to understand is to love. Whereas to hate is not to understand at all. If we remain receptive and learn to read and see in better ways (practice makes perfect here, too), we are likely to find that Hollywood produces lots of values worth having or at least contemplating. And the big surprise will come when we discover that many of these values in question are actually traditional or even classic values. What I aim to do in this book is to explore a certain number of movies along these lines, movies that throw light on education (as opposed to indoctrination), on the many faces of love, on the vicissitudes of fighting for truth and justice, and on the often difficult enterprise of really making a difference.

Movies, like plays or novels or even poems, can be historical or philosophical, theological or psychological, or even sociological in their import. They can be deeply moving as well as entertaining, entertaining especially perhaps when they are also deeply moving. They speak to us from the depths of our humanity to the depths of our humanity. I have yet to see a movie from which I have learned nothing at all. And I am looking forward to seeing many more, always on the look-out for useful and insightful "messages" that I can translate into my ever-growing pleasure in understanding both myself and my fellow human beings. We are in this together. And how we treat each other and each other's thoughts and feelings can make all the difference in the world. Shall we go to the movies then?

Chapter One

Hollywood Goes to School

1. Dead Poets Society

[Movie Log: Released in 1989 by Touchstone Pictures. Screenplay by Tom Schulman. Directed by Peter Weir. Cast: Robin Williams (John Keating); Robert Sean Leonard (Neil Perry); Ethan Hawke (Todd Anderson); Josh Charles (Knox Overstreet); Gale Hansen (Charles Dalton); Dylan Kussman (Richard Cameron); Norman Lloyd (Mr. Nolan); Kurtwood Smith (Mr. Perry)]

> *Cursed be the social wants that sin against the strength of youth!*
> *Cursed by the social lies that wrap us from the living truth!*
> —Alfred Lord Tennyson, "Locksley Hall"

> *Perhaps adolescent students are often impervious to the appeal of literature because for them words do not represent keen sensuous, emotional, and intellectual perceptions. This indicates that throughout the entire course of their education, the element of personal insight and experience has been neglected for verbal abstractions...The history of criticism is peopled with writers who possess refined taste but who remain minor critics precisely because they are minor personalities, limited in their understanding of life. Knowledge of literary forms is empty without an accompanying humanity.*
> —Louis M. Rosenblatt, *Literature as Exploration*

The ceremonies that open the new school year of 1959-60 at Welton Academy in Vermont are reminiscent of a church service. There is, of course, nothing wrong with such ceremonies, nor can we find fault with the "four pillars" of the school, "Tradition, Honor, Discipline, Excellence." The immediate aftermath of the opening ceremonies continues the church-service feel. Mr. Nolan, the headmaster, stands in the doorway shaking hands with the parents of returning students who compliment him for the "thrilling" or "lovely ceremony" he has just

1

performed. It is also here, during the opening ceremonies, that the new English teacher, John Keating, is introduced to the student body.

As we witness the hustle and bustle of students settling in, certain students emerge from the nameless crowd as young men who will play a prominent role in the story. Among these are Neil Perry and his new roommate, Todd Anderson. Though John Keating, their English teacher, is in some sense the hero of this film, the story really belongs, in a sense, to Neil and Todd. The other students who figure in an important way in the story include Knox Overstreet and Charles Dalton as well as Richard Cameron. Cameron quickly shows himself as possibly the most conformist among the circle of friends who occupy our center of attention, and Mr. Perry, Neil's father also quickly emerges as the instigator of a conflict in the story that will ultimately have tragic consequences.

Mr. Perry comes up to Neil's room (to the surprise of all the students present) and tells him that he has talked to Mr. Nolan and has decided that Neil has taken on too many extracurricular activities and that he is to drop his assistant editorship of the school annual. It is clear from the beginning, therefore, that Mr. Perry is adamant about Neil's progress towards a future that only he, Mr. Perry, envisions for him. Thus Charlie Dalton's innocent-sounding question ("Why doesn't he let you do what you want?") is replete with ominous implications this early in the game.

In what follows we get three quick glimpses into the routine of Welton Academy. We see, for a moment, students in the chemistry lab followed by a Latin class followed by a math class. The next class is English. And it is here that we get our first real introduction to John Keating. He enters the class whistling a tune from Tchaikovsky's "1812 Overture," walks to the back of the room and goes out into the hallway. He sticks his head back into the classroom and invites the puzzled students to follow him. The first words out of his mouth are "O Captain, My Captain," the opening line of a Whitman poem about Lincoln's death (in light of what is to follow, this choice is more telling than its immediate significance—that is, as a possible nickname for John Keating himself).

Keating's first act of business is to ask one of the students to read the first four lines of Robert Herrick's "To the Virgins, to Make Much of Time," the most famous "carpe diem" or "seize the day" poem in English: "Gather ye rosebuds while ye may: / Old time is still a-flying; / And this same flower that smiles today, / Tomorrow will be dying." Keating follows this up with a reminder that we are "food for worms." This is a somewhat unorthodox invocation of the time-honored adage about life being too short, though it may certainly be appropriate for a teacher to use this perhaps unusual but highly effective method to drive home the point that young people are only young for a "short" time and that they should thus make the most of their time by seizing the day, thus making their "lives extraordinary." The fact that all this takes place in front of a class picture of a long-ago student body on the wall (the members of which are by this time probably all dead) just delivers the point Keating is making with that much more relevance and effectiveness.

The students seem delighted with Keating's ways. The only exception appears to be Cameron. When he asks "Think he will test us on that stuff?" Charlie Dalton aptly replies "Don't you get anything?" Later it will be Cameron again who will be most reluctant to tear out the pages from the textbook on poetry at Keating's request and who will later still have doubts about renewing the Dead Poets Society Keating was a part of when he was a student at Welton Academy. In the scene where Keating asks the students to tear the pages out of their textbook we witness the second major scene involving Keating's ingenious and most effective teaching methods. Part of the secret of Keating's success with his students is, of course, the fact that he levels with them, that he tells them (and occasionally shows them, too) what he firmly believes to be the truth.

The essay, "Understanding Poetry," by J. Evans Pritchard, Ph.D., is indeed "excrement" (to use Keating's own characterization of it). The "greatness" of a poem is not to be grafted onto horizontal and vertical lines where the first represents the "perfection" (as to rhythm, meter, and rhyme) and the second the "importance" (as to theme) of a given poem. As Keating tells the students after they have torn the offending pages from the book, "[w]e don't read and write poetry because it's cute. We read and write poetry because we are members of the human race. And the human race is filled with passion. Medicine, law, business, engineering, these are all noble pursuits, and necessary to sustain life. But poetry, beauty, romance, love, these are what we stay alive for."

With Neil's discovery of Keating's senior annual, the old Dead Poets Society that Keating was involved with when he was a student at Welton (Hellton, by nickname) rears its head. The students, who are naturally curious, ask Keating about it. He tells them how a group of them used to get together at the "old Indian cave" and "in the enchantment of the moment ... let poetry work its magic." When Knox has doubts about a bunch of guys just "sitting around reading poetry," Keating claims that they were not just a "Greek organization," that they "were romantics," that they "didn't just read poetry" but "let it drip from [their] tongues like honey. Spirits soared, women swooned and gods were created, gentlemen. Not a bad way to spend an evening."

That evening, under Neil's leadership, the boys "reconvene" the Dead Poets Society. As usual, the only student who worries about this "underground" activity is Cameron. Neil honors tradition by opening the new "chapter" of the society the way Keating and his classmates used to open it, by reading from Henry David Thoreau's *Walden* the passage about "going to the woods" in order to "live deliberately," to "live deep and suck out the marrow of life," so that when they came "to die" they would not "discover" that they "had not lived" at all. This first meeting of the renewed society is a tremendous success. The boys really get into reading poetry, reciting it with gusto, including the concluding lines from Tennyson's "Ulysses," which Neil reads and which, in the context of the movie as a whole, conjures up a special significance:

> Come my friends. 'Tis not too late to seek
> A newer world, for my purpose holds
> To sail beyond the sunset... And tho'
> We are not that strength which in old days
> Moved earth and heaven,
> That which we are, we are—
> One equal temper of heroic hearts,
> Made weak by time and fate, but strong in will
> To strive, to seek, to find, and not to yield.

It is as if the splendor of these words, spoken by an aged Ulysses in the poem itself, performed a double function by reflecting both on Keating's generation of the past and that of Neil's and his classmates in the present. There is indeed "tradition, honor, discipline, and excellence" in this student-led initiative to revive the Dead Poets Society, in spite of the fact that (as Keating himself puts it) the school's "present administration" would not approve it.

It is in the next classroom scene that Keating performs his famous stunt of standing upon the desk to remind the students that they "must constantly look at things in a different way." "Just when you think you know something," he tells them a moment later, "you have to look at it in another way." He urges them to think when they read and "not just [think] what the author thinks. Consider what you think" as well. He urges them, too, to find their own voices. There is no time to waste. The more habitual their thinking becomes, the more difficult it will be to change it. It is interesting to reflect in this connection that both George McAllister, a fellow teacher, and Mr. Nolan object (the first mildly, the second vehemently) to Keating's attempt to make 17-year-olds think for themselves.

The "magic" of Keating's teaching soon begins to show results. It encourages Knox to "woo" Chris (who is engaged to a "jerk" of a football player) to "seize the day" and not to give up prematurely (we should recall in this connection, too, that—as Keating tells the students at one point—language was invented not in order to let us communicate, but in order to "woo women"), and it enables Neil to let his own hidden ambition to become an actor come forth. Once Neil decides upon trying out for a role in Shakespeare's *Midsummer Night's Dream*, he bubbles over with joy and enthusiasm:

> So, I am gonna act. Yes, yes! I am gonna be an actor! Ever since I can remember, I've wanted to try this. I even tried to go to summer stock auditions last year, but, of course, my father wouldn't let me. For the first time in my whole life I know what I wanna do, and for the first time I am gonna do it whether my father wants me to or not! Carpe diem!

Neil knows that his father would be adamantly opposed to his ambition to become and actor, so when he gets the part of Puck, he forges a letter of permission in his father's name. In the meantime, Mr. Keating continues to encourage the students to be their own persons. In order to illustrate the dangers of conformity, for example, he lets them march until they begin to step in unison on the school's grounds in a location where Mr. Nolan happens to be able to observe what goes on. Keating tells the students that while they each started out with "their own stride, their own pace," they soon began to conform. He tells them how difficult it is to maintain one's beliefs against opposition from others. He tells them, too, that while we have a "great need for acceptance," we should nevertheless try to strive to be ourselves even in the face of the disapproval of the "herd." He ends by quoting Robert Frost's famous lines: "Two roads diverged in a wood and I, / I took the one less traveled by, / And that has made all the difference."

In the meantime Charlie Dalton brings two girls to one of the Dead Poets Society meetings, where he also owns up to having written a surreptitious article for the school paper "demanding that girls be admitted to Welton." Though the group as a whole objects to Charlie's having taken upon himself to "speak for the club," it is Cameron, once more, who is really worried about what the administration is likely to do about this mischievous breach of conduct. When Mr. Nolan insists that whoever is responsible for the "profane and unauthorized article" reveal himself on pain of expulsion from the school, Charlie adds insult to injury by pretending to receive a phone call from God whose message to Mr. Nolan is that "we should have girls at Welton."

In the scene that follows Mr. Nolan administers a rather nasty paddling upon Charlie Dalton's backside while demanding to know what the Dead Poets Society is and also by demanding "names." As Charlie later tells Neil and others, it appears that if he turns everybody in and apologizes to the school as a whole "all will be forgiven." It is after this scene that Mr. Nolan pulls Mr. Keating aside for a little talk. Nolan tells Keating about "rumors" concerning his "unorthodox teaching methods." And while Nolan doesn't blame Keating for the stunt that Charlie pulled, he does want to know what the boys were doing "marching, and clapping in unison" a bit earlier.

To Keating's explanation that the "exercise" was to "prove a point" about the "dangers of conformity," Nolan responds with, "Well, John, the curriculum here is set. It's proven it works. If you question [it], what's to prevent them from doing the same?" "I always thought," responds Keating, that "the idea of educating was to learn to think for yourself." "At these boys' ages? Not on your life!" exclaims Nolan. "Tradition, John. Discipline. Prepare them for college, and the rest will take care of itself."

Though not in agreement with the administration on many issues, Keating nevertheless reprimands Charlie Dalton for the stunt he has pulled. He reminds the student that "sucking the marrow out of life doesn't mean choking on the bone." With the jocular reminder that one of the consequences of being expelled from Welton would be that Charlie could no longer take Keating's courses, the student sees the point. "Aye, aye, Captain," he says.

6

In the meantime it seems that Mr. Perry has gotten a wind of Neil's newly launched acting career. He is, of course, dead set against Neil's continued association with the play. He also suspects that "this new man," this, "ah, Mr. Keating" may have put him up to it. In any event, regardless of the fact that Neil has a leading role in the play, which is to open the day after, Mr. Perry orders his son to quit immediately. He doesn't care, as he says, "if the world comes to an end," Neil must be "through with [the] play."

Neil now turns to the one person he is sure will understand his dilemma, Mr. Keating. In a private conference Neil tells his teacher that his father wants him to quit the play, that he is "planning the rest of [his] life for [him]," that he has never "asked [him]" what he (Neil) wanted. Keating wants Neil to talk to his father, to tell him how he feels. But Neil says that he "can't talk to him this way" (that is, the way in which he can tall to Keating). Keating nevertheless urges Neil to talk again to his father in order to be able to stay in the play. The next time they see each other, Neil lies to Keating by saying that he has, in fact, talked to his father who, though reluctantly, has agreed to let him remain in the play.

Though Mr. Perry is not supposed to be at the play (he is supposed to be in Chicago), he does walk into the auditorium and stands in the back as the play comes to a close. Neil as Puck sees him and then seems to address the play's epilogue to his father as well as to the audience so that the final words of the play take on a special and unique significance in what thus becomes a private/public context:

> If we shadows have offended,
> Think but this, and all is mended,
> That you have but slumber'd here
> While these visions did appear.
> And this weak and idle theme,
> No more yielding but a dream,
> Gentles, do no reprehend;
> If you pardon, we will mend;
> And, as I am an honest Puck,
> If we have unearned luck
> Now to 'scape the serpent's tongue,
> We will make amends ere long;
> Else the Puck a liar call;

> So, good night unto you all.
> Give me your hands, if we be friends,
> And Robin shall restore amends.

But Puck/Neil's final words fall upon deaf ears as far as his father is concerned. When after the play Keating (as well as all the students) congratulate Neil on his magnificent performance, Mr. Perry rudely tells Keating to "stay away from [his] son." Having forcefully dragged him home, Mr. Perry, as if speaking on behalf of Mrs. Perry (who looks on in apparent despair) as well as in his own right, tells Neil in no uncertain terms that he is to go to military school immediately and then to Harvard where he is to study medicine. Mr. Perry completely disregards his son's wishes and browbeats the latter to the point where Neil simply gives up even to try to get his father to let him be what *he* wants to be.

During the quiet of the cold winter night, in front of an open window, Neil seems to enact a strange ritual with what appears to be a crown of thorns on his head (a stage prop left over from his role as Puck), while he exposes his naked body to the elements. He then quietly walks down to a study where, pulling a handgun from what is apparently his father's desk, he shoots himself dead. The sound of the gunshot awakens Mr. Perry who immediately goes searching for his son by walking from room to room in the house, followed by Mrs. Perry. When he stumbles upon the body, he cries out repeatedly, "Oh, Neil! Oh, My God! ... Oh, my son! ... My son! My poor son!"

When Charlie informs Todd of Neil's death, they all run out into the wintry night where it is Todd who repeatedly says that it was Neil's father who killed him. The context of his words (Neil "wouldn't have left us... His father killed him") seems to imply that Mr. Perry had, in fact, literally killed his own son. In a way, of course, it is clear to us all that he is, above all, the most responsible for Neil's death, for it is clear that Neil felt totally "trapped" (a word he actually uses when talking to Keating about his father wanting him to quit the play), that he felt that his father was simply forcing him, against his will and against all of his heart's desires, to go to military and then to medical school.

Yet now, in spite of what we (as audience) know, the film takes a turn for a perhaps predictable but ultimately unjustifiable assignment of blame. When Mr. Nolan announces that he "intend[s] to conduct a thorough inquiry into this matter," we may already guess that Mr. Keating will

8

emerge as the villain in the eyes of official justice and established morality. Cameron is, of course, the first to "fink." And when one of the students wants to know what Cameron could possibly fink about, Charlie Dalton hits the nail right on the proverbial head:

> The club...Think about it. The board of directors, the trustees, Mr. Nolan. Do you think for one moment they're gonna let this thing just blow over? Schools go down because of things like this. They need a scapegoat.

Cameron has the unmitigated audacity to speak of the school's "honor code" when he admits that he has, in fact, "finked." He tells the others that if they are smart, they will do as he did. "They are not after us. We are the victims. Us and Neil." When Charlie wants to know who they are after, Cameron says, in no uncertain terms, "Mr. Keating, of course. The 'Captain' himself. I mean, you guys didn't really think he could avoid responsibility, did you?" When Charlie is horrified by the suggestion that Mr. Keating is to be blamed for Neil's suicide, Cameron continues:

> Well, who else do you think, dumb-ass? The administration? Mr. Perry? Mr. Keating put us up to all this crap, didn't he? If it wasn't for Mr. Keating, Neil would be cozied up in his room right now, studying his chemistry and dreaming of being called a doctor.

This misleading and illogical explanation, the falseness of which Todd, for example, vehemently objects to ("That is not true, Cameron. You know that. He didn't put us up to anything. Neil loved acting") will nonetheless become the official explanation as well. In the scene in which Todd, for example, is "interrogated" (in the presence of his parents) by Mr. Nolan, and then made to sign a "document" (the scene is reminiscent of phony confessions that prisoners, after having been tortured, were forced to sign in the former Soviet Union), Mr. Nolan says:

> I have here a detailed description of what occurred at your meetings. It describes how your teacher, Mr. Keating, encouraged you boys to organize this club and to use it as a source of inspiration for reckless and self-indulgent behavior. It describes how Mr. Keating, both in and out of the classroom, encouraged

Neil Perry to follow his obsession with acting when he knew all along it was against the explicit order of Neil's parents. It was Mr. Keating's blatant abuse of his position as teacher that led directly to Neil Perry's death.

Needless to say, this highly distorted version becomes, as I have said before, the official view of what has led to Neil's suicide. The upshot of the whole affair is that in the end things are back to normal at Welton Academy. When Mr. Keating, who has obviously been dismissed, comes for his "personals," Mr. Nolan is in charge of his class. And the students are asked to start all over again by reading what Mr. Nolan calls the "excellent essay by Dr. Pritchard on 'Understanding Poetry.'" It is Cameron who explains that the pages of the essay have been torn out of the book, so he is forced to read the essay in question from Mr. Nolan's own copy.

As Mr. Keating is about to leave the classroom, Todd exclaims that "they made everybody sign" the document leading to Keating's dismissal. When Todd jumps up on his desk to the exclamation of "O Captain! My Captain!" and when other students follow suit, it becomes apparent that Mr. Nolan is not going to be able to maintain control of the class. In the end, only a handful of students remain seated (including, of course, Cameron), the rest are on their desks shouting "O Captain! My Captain!" The students thus undo the injustice imposed upon Mr. Keating by the administration, but not officially. That is beyond their power. The movie nevertheless ends on a note of moral triumph. The taste of bitterness and sadness which remain with us as we witness Mr. Keating, with tears of gratitude in his eyes, say "Thank you, boys. Thank you," reminds me not just of the "four pillars" of Welton Academy (Tradition. Honor. Discipline. Excellence), but also of the parody of this we hear early on in the story, shortly after the opening ceremonies: "Travesty. Horror. Decadence. Excrement." Those words in the end are indeed better at describing what has happened not just to Mr. Keating in this case, but to all the students who have thus been deprived of a truly dedicated and brilliant teacher.

What this movie tells us—nay, what it *shows* us—is that excellence is not always rewarded in our world, that discipline is at times nothing more than the rigid application of misguided and illogical distortions, that honor can be horribly twisted to suit dishonorable ends, and that thus tradition may indeed become its own travesty. When will we ever learn? And why not in school, of all places?

2. Patch Adams

[Movie Log: Rleased in 1998 by Universal Pictures. Screenplay by Steve Oedekerk, based on *Gesundheit:Good Health is a Laughing Matter*, by Hunter Doherty Adams. Directed by Tom Shadyac. Cast: Robin Williams (Hunter "Patch" Adams); Monica Potter (Carin Fisher); Truman Schiff (Daniel London); Philip Seymour Hoffman (Mitch); Bob Gunton (Dean Walcott); Harve Presnell (Dean Anderson); Harold Gould (Arthur Mandelson); Michael Jeter (Rudy)]

> *It has crossed my mind to wonder whether it isn't the point of all professions—of medicine and law as much as of philosophy and psychoanalysis—to instill deadness. Of course, the conscious self-image of every profession is that it is there to maintain high standards. And there must be some truth in this image. But what does this image cover over? Don't standards themselves impose a kind of rigidity on a practice? Doesn't a professional set of standards enable a profession to forget about standards? That is, it enables a profession to stop thinking critically about how it ought to go on precisely because the standards present themselves as having already answered the question. The profession can then act as though it already knows what high standards are. This is a form of deadness.*
> —Jonathan Lear, *Open Minded: Working out the Logic of the Soul*

The book from which my opening quotation is taken happens to have been published in the same year in which *Patch Adams* was released. Though the connection between the publication of the book and the release of the movie is undoubtedly purely coincidental, the thematic similarity between the passage quoted and *Patch Adams* is astounding. It is indeed in our best interest both to honor the tradition within which we ply our trade and to challenge it from time to time in order to keep it vital. There is a danger in honoring tradition blindly and making sure that it remains unchanged no matter what. We must at times unthink our thinking

11

lest our thinking become unthinking thinking, for the enemy of critical thinking is habitual ways of thinking. Those who are convinced that they already have all the answers are not the best representatives of a given profession.

As Arthur Mendelson tells Hunter Adams at the time he renames him Patch, it is incumbent upon us to see what no one else sees, because by merely focusing on a problem, we may well overlook its solution. As with the puzzle of the four fingers, knowing the "right [read: settled once and for all] answer" isn't always possible in "real life." Which is precisely why the official view of things must be challenged from time to time, for officially accepted views of things (even officially accepted versions of truth and justice) aren't necessarily so (or either true or just). There are times when tradition is a dead weight unnecessarily burdening the living, those who are made to carry it. Even if it doesn't kill us, it will slow us down and make us overlook the possibility of throwing it off, of being liberated from it. It is also interesting to note that Patch gets his new name when he repairs a leaking paper cup with a piece of self-adhesive strip that was originally meant for another purpose.

The opening words of the movie ("All life is a coming home"), should remind us of the *Odyssey*, the ultimate coming home story in classical literature. But in this context the words express something more than a literal return home, they express something like having found one's true place in the world. Patch also invokes the opening words of Dante's *Inferno* when he speaks of having lost the right path in the middle of his life's journey—the right path, which he was to find eventually "in the most unlikely place," in a psychiatric ward. What unfolds here is a clear statement of the overall theme of the movie as a whole. We see this when we witness the injection in the buttocks that Rudy receives when he acts hysterically, as if this were the only solution to his problem. And we also see this when we realize that the psychologist is not listening to Patch as the latter recounts his father's death and how his world had changed as a result of that event.

The true solution to Rudy's problem, his unduly fear of squirrels (because they may be after his "nuts"—one of the first in a series of many word plays and puns in the movie as a whole), is something that Patch accidentally stumbles upon when, partly for the sake of his own convenience, he decides to enter into Rudy's delusion and starts shooting the imaginary (but to Rudy very real) squirrels with equally imaginary guns. It is, paradoxically, by taking Rudy's delusion seriously that Patch manages to "cure" Rudy of it. Clearly what Rudy needed was not injections in the buttocks, but someone to understand what it was that he had been afraid of in the first place.

Contrary to what Patch says later (about how it wasn't the doctors that helped him, but the patients), it is really Patch who helps himself, albeit indirectly. As he puts it later, by concentrating on the problems of others, he forgot about his own. What he discovers is that God doesn't necessarily help those who help themselves, that God may well help those who help others. Thus at times it is only by helping others that we can truly help ourselves. But this isn't possible if we don't listen to our fellow human beings, if we won't pay attention to what is really bothering them. Merely being paid to help others (as in the case with the psychologist who doesn't listen to Patch) will not do the trick, even if the person being paid is an otherwise well-trained professional. Patch is right when he tells the doctor on the morning of his departure from Fairfax Hospital that the doctor "sucks" at helping others because he doesn't "listen, really listen to people."

When the story picks up two years later at Virginia Medical University, Dean Walcott is lecturing. His theme is the time-honored "do no harm" of the medical profession (part of the Hippocratic oath), but his reason for advocating it is grounded in a kind of misanthropy, an attempt to undo the seemingly natural trust that people place in doctors, because no human being, according to Dean Walcott, is worthy of trust. It is, therefore, as he tells his students, his ambition to "train the humanity out of [them], to make [them] into something better." Although Dean Walcott's message is clear enough as far as what he is trying impart to his students about the medical profession is concerned, there is an unwelcome implication in the idea that doctors, if they are to be any good, must be better than human beings, must somehow transcend and stay aloof of their own humanity. The entire class applauds Dean Walcott's lecture enthusiastically, only Patch Adams seems unmoved and without a smile on his face.

Carin Fisher reinforces Dean Walcott's message when she tells Patch, who is trying to engage her in conversation after the lecture (it seems he has been instantly smitten by her), that she is there to study medicine, period. Later, in the University Diner, where Patch has gone with his newly-made friend, Truman Schiff, the two talk about the ways in which society turns spontaneous individuals with open minds into robots apparently not capable of anything but programmed responses. Patch is convinced, though, that the program can be changed. After an attempt to prove this (by suddenly dropping down head first from the branch of a tree on the sidewalk, for example, which at first scares an elderly woman but then, after a bit of delay, makes her respond favorably to the joke), Patch and Truman get quite accidentally caught up with a bunch of meat packers who are having a convention nearby.

The purpose of the episode with the meat packers is twofold. It gives us a chance to see just how spontaneous and funny Patch can be, but it also enables us to see him suddenly realize that, in a way, what stands in his way of engaging with patients is a white coat (which third-year medical students wear in their hospital rounds). Patch uses the coat the meat packers give him in lieu of a doctor's traditional white coat. And his first act of imposture is to inquire after the name of a frightened diabetic woman suddenly surrounded by a bunch of medical students in white coats who are there to observe her from a strictly objective and professional (read: totally impersonal) point of view. As the students move on, Patch squeezes the woman's hand as a gesture of human touch, which has already become his trademark, both in a literal and in a figurative sense.

It is in order to avoid getting caught by Dean Walcott that Patch stumbles into the children's cancer wing where he first puts on the red enema bulb as his clown's nose. The sleepy, morose children in the deathly quiet ward soon respond to Patch's antics so that laughter quickly fills the room, which then almost instantly turns into a state of joyous pandemonium. It is as if for a few moments at least the children forgot where they were and why. In the scene immediately following this, we see Patch in Dean Walcott's office as the latter "lectures" him about people with brilliant minds who don't think that the rules apply to them. It is here that he tells Patch that "passion doesn't make doctors," that the likes of him—that is, the likes of Dean Walcott— "make doctors." When Patch wants to know why things have to be the way they are, Dean Walcott's simple response is the usual and rather predictable "our way of doing things is a product of centuries of experience." No doubt.

"Deviation of the tongue," says a member of the study group sitting around a table in the library. One cannot help but think that this transition from Walcott's office to the scene in the library is well punctuated by a "deviation of the tongue," for (indeed) it seems that someone somewhere has misspoken something. The irony implicit in the title of the book Patch holds in his hands in this scene should not escape the viewer either: *The Business of Medicine*. Of course, the word "business" can function in multiple ways, but (again) one cannot help but feel that the medical profession was never meant to be simply a business, like any other business, in business for profit and profit alone (the Hippocratic oath makes this very clear, too). At this point Carin once more rebuffs Patch when the latter seems more interested in discussing *why* people want to become doctors than the biology lesson immediately at hand, the "deviation of the tongue."

What follows is a series of pranks in which Patch in one way or another is trying to drive home the lesson that "laughter is the best medicine." Carin is not buying any of this at first, but when she sees the grades posted on the wall in the hallway and realizes that Patch's grades are among the highest in the class, she begins to waver. Indeed, all those reviews of the movie that pan Patch on the grounds that they want serious doctors rather than clowns overlook not only the whole point of the movie but also the fact that Patch is not simply a clown but also a serious and highly competent doctor-to-be who, in addition to all the other qualifications any doctor may need, also has a sense of humor and believes that a touch of humanity is never out of place in the healing profession. In any event, Carin is now ready to assist Patch in yet another prank to cheer up one of the patients. Patch's antics usually pay off, except in the case (an admittedly difficult case) of Mr. Davis, a patient dying of pancreatic cancer. Patch doesn't give up, though. He goes to Room 305 at one point dressed as an angel and finally manages to get through to Mr. Davis with a series of word plays, colloquial euphemisms for dying, and puns on a "preview of coming attractions."

In spite of repeated warnings from Dean Walcott (who firmly believes that "patients don't need to be entertained. They don't need a friend, they need a doctor"), Patch goes on with his antics. When he is put in charge of the welcoming committee for the "medical seminar/retreat for the fellowship of the American College of Gynecologists," Patch outdoes himself. The gigantic papier-mâché legs spread out on either side of a doorway, which thus functions as a vagina (a huge pun on the birth canal through which the visiting gynecologists are to enter the auditorium), proves too much for Dean Walcott. He uses this attempt at humor on

15

Patch's part to dismiss him from school. It is only because his antics have obviously improved the patients at the hospital that Dean Anderson overrides Dean Walcott's decision and allows Patch to stay in school.

In the meantime, though still wary, Carin is more and more responsive to Patch's larger than life humanity. This becomes especially obvious when Patch throws her a surprise birthday party where, in the balloon-filled room, he begins to read to her the opening lines from one of Pablo Neruda's love sonnets, which he is not going to be able to finish until much later, in rather sad circumstances. The opening lines of the poem are:

> I do not love you as if you were salt-rose, or topaz,
> or the arrow of carnations the fire shoots off.
> I love you as certain dark things are to be loved,
> in secret ...

When Patch encounters a frantic woman who is not allowed to see her dying daughter (the victim of a drunk driver who has already taken her son and husband), because she hasn't filled out certain forms yet, he is ready to act. It is in the University Diner that he suddenly sees what he needs and wants to do, to create a free clinic where bureaucracy never stands in the way of people helping people. As Patch tells Carin, he wants this to be the "first fun hospital in the world" where "love is the ultimate goal." To the still skeptical Carin he says that "there is more to life than power and control." Carin's "people get hurt" remark carries an ominous ring. Patch sympathizes with her and wants to know who it was that hurt her.

When the Gesundheit Institute opens out in the countryside in the midst of imposingly verdant mountains (thanks to Arthur Mendelson's generosity who owns this particular piece of land), everything seems right with the world. So much so that Carin's final reservations are broken down as, one evening on the steps in front of their newly renovated building, she confides in Patch about a troubled childhood (it seems she has been victimized by men in a sexual way early on in her life) and admits that she loves him. The only thing they don't see eye-to-eye about is a certain suicidal person, Larry by name (whom we have already seen briefly in the emergency room after one of his attempted suicides). Carin thinks he is "weird" in an unseemly kind of way. Patch ignores her premonition.

When late one evening Larry calls wanting to talk to someone, Carin responds by going over to his house. Larry is seated at the piano in his ornate living room playing Beethoven's "Für Elise" when Carin arrives. He has inherited this house from his father, who died two years earlier and whose death is apparently at the root of his suicidal tendencies. As he closes the door of the closet into which he has just placed Carin's coat, the screen goes dark. The next thing we know is that Patch is called to Dean Anderson's office who informs him that Carin was murdered the night before.

Patch's world now falls apart. He blames himself for Carin's death. As he says later, "I taught her the medicine that killed her." At the funeral, when the service has ended and when everyone else has departed, Patch stands with tearful eyes by Carin's coffin and finishes reading the poem he has begun to read at Carin's surprise birthday party in the balloon-filled room. He has attempted to finish the poem on a previous occasion, the morning after Carin had confided in him and confessed her love for him. During the evening in question Carin spoke of her childhood envy of caterpillars which could "turn into beautiful creatures that could fly away untouched." The morning following this magical evening we see Carin still asleep in her bed under a window in the middle of which is the large stained-glass image of a butterfly. Patch stands over her bed and reads a few more words from the poem: "I love you without knowing how, or when, or from where..." Now at her coffin Patch finally reads the concluding lines of the poem ("I love you straightforwardly, without complexities or pride; / So I love you because I know no other way / than this: where *I* does not exist, nor *you*, / so close that your hand on my chest is my hand, / so close that your eyes close as I fall asleep"), after which, his eyes full of tears, he kisses the coffin in desperation, as if kissing Carin for one last time.

Though both Truman and Mitch, his roommate and former nemesis, urge Patch not to give up, Patch's heart is no longer in his vision for a better world in which hospitals are places of fun as well as places of healing. He goes up to the mountain where the Gesundheit Institute is located and, standing on top of a cliff, he obviously contemplates suicide as he accuses God of having rested on the seventh day of creation instead of devoting it to compassion. As he turns back from the abyss, he sees a butterfly land on his old leather case. The butterfly then lights on his chest, where his heart is. Then it lands on his hand whence it flies away. The implication is that this butterfly (a traditional symbol of the soul) is Carin's spirit or at least her emissary.

The visit to the mountain top refreshes Patch's revolve to go on with life as a doctor-to-be. He now helps Mitch with Mrs. Kennedy (who wouldn't eat) to fulfill a fantasy of hers to splash about it a pool filled with "noodles." But things are not getting back to normal. Dean Walcott strikes. Patch is threatened by expulsion on the grounds of practicing medicine without a license. At his trial in front of the State Medical Board he speaks eloquently in his own defense. The room is filled with people who are rooting for him. He tells the panel of doctors sitting in judgment of him that if "you treat a disease, you win, you lose," but that if "you treat a person, you win, no matter what the outcome." During his impassioned defense he turns around to address his fellow students in the balcony. He urges them not to let themselves "be anesthetized," not to let themselves be "numbed out." Prior to the verdict, the children from the cancer wing come and put on red noses in a show of solidarity. When the doctors return from their brief deliberations, they tell Patch that, although they disagree with some of his methods, they can "find no fault" with his passion for his patients. They assert that he carries with him a "flame, which one could only hope would spread through the medical profession like a brushfire." And they also tell Dean Walcott that he need not bring Patch's case in front of a tribunal again but that he ought to perhaps himself practice a bit of "excessive happiness."

The story concludes with the graduation ceremonies that make, among other things, Hunter "Patch" Adams a doctor. Viewers may think that mooning the audience (which laughs with delight) as well as the august professors up on the stage is a bit much, but upon further reflection it may simply be a final confirmation of what is really important. Clearly, it is not merely academic gowns and degrees. Nor is it merely the time-honored title of "doctor of medicine." Rather it is what the gowns and the degrees and the titles are for. They are not ends in themselves. They are means to a greater end. What Patch's mooning makes fun of is our tendency to allow the trappings of what we do to take precedence over the essence, the heart of the matter. Such a reminder, vulgar as it may strike some, is healthy to the core (no pun intended). And that's what this movie is all about, how to be healthy to the core not just in a literal but in a metaphorical sense as well.

3. Lean On Me

[Movie Log: Released in 1989 by Warner Bros. Screenplay by Michael Schiffer. Directed by John G. Avildsen. Cast: Morgan Freeman (Joe Clark); Beverly Todd (Ms. Levias); Robert Guillaume (Dr. Frank Napier); Sandra Reaves-Phillips (Mrs. Powers); Jermaine Hopkins (Thomas Sams); Karen Malina White (Kaneesha Carter); Alan North (Mayor Bottman); Lynn Thigpen (Leonna Barrett)]

> *Not he is great who can alter matter, but he who can alter my state of mind.*
> —Ralph Waldo Emerson, "The American Scholar"

Based on a true story, *Lean On Me* can teach us a great deal about the problematic mix between politics and education as well as about the politics of education itself. It also highlights the importance of personal involvement as opposed to merely doing the best you can, given the circumstances. Before the credits roll, we are in Joe Clark's classroom in 1967. He is a "hip" teacher who runs his classes as game shows, whipping his students into enthusiasm with his energetic and dynamic approach. But there is trouble at Eastside High in Paterson, New Jersey. The Union Executive Board, under pressure from the Board of Education, agrees to transfer "Crazy" Joe Clark to another school. When Joe Clark calls them Judases (who "sell out every time" the Board of Education threatens them—and money is the bottom line), we get the first of a series of references that give the story a kind of religious undercurrent (more of this later).

When the credits roll the story picks up 20 years later. The halls of Eastside High are now filled with debris and unseemly graffiti, the visible signs of violence and drugs. A girl is attacked in the restroom, a fight breaks out and a person is taken away on a stretcher. We almost get the impression that this sorry state of affairs is, in a way, the direct result of transferring the likes of Joe Clark from Eastside High 20 years before. Perhaps the point the movie is trying to make this early in the game is that if teachers don't have control over how and what they teach, they may well end up losing control of their students. And losing control of their students is paramount to losing control of the school as a whole. These troubles, of course, extend beyond the walls of the school. We are next in the mayor's office where the school's lawyer, in the company of Superintendent Napier, informs the mayor that unless 75 percent of the student body at Eastside High can pass the state's basic skills test, the state will take over the school. (The last time the test was given less than one third of the student body has managed this feat.)

It is here that Dr. Frank Napier, an old friend and colleague of Joe Clark, suggests that they need a principal who has "nothing to lose" by trying to turn the school around. City Hall would benefit by this, too, so here we also see a connection between politics and education, a connection that has nothing to do with learning per se, but with reputation and budgetary considerations. The mayor agrees to Joe Clark's appointment but mutters "God help us" under his breath. Frank Napier and the school's lawyer go to see Joe Clark who is now the principal of an elementary school in a nice neighborhood. Joe Clark's first reaction is not to accept the position on the grounds that it's being offered to him as a mere political maneuver on the part of both the mayor and the superintendent of schools. But Frank Napier gives Joe Clark a challenge he can't refuse. He asks him what he has ever done in his life that has really made a difference. Joe Clark finds this challenge irresistible. Perhaps the easiest way of life isn't necessarily the best.

As soon as he arrives at Eastside High he takes over the helm with the most forceful and commanding attitude. He makes it clear at the outset to the teachers and staff that from that moment on business is not going to be as usual. He wants a list of "every hoodlum, drug dealer and miscreant," he wants the cages in the cafeteria torn down ("if you treat them like animals, they'll behave like animals"), and he asserts, in no uncertain terms, that "this is an institution of learning, ladies and gentlemen, if you can't control it, how can you teach?" He also asserts that "discipline is not the enemy of enthusiasm" and, because of how bad things have gotten, things will not be the way they used to be, the school is no longer a "democracy." Since they are in a "state of emergency," Joe Clark's word will be "law." All this control may not strike the viewers as perhaps desirable, but such sentiments may really be irrelevant for the time being. Business as usual has not done the trick; the school has deteriorated into chaos where learning is virtually impossible. Part of the "message" of this movie is that there may indeed be times when the ends must justify the means (and it would be a mistake to assume that this is advocated as a general rule, it is only necessary when there seems to be no other workable alternative).

It takes Joe Clark some time before he can gain control of the students' attention in assembly. The "hoodlums" and "drug dealers" have been asked to ascend the stage of the auditorium. Joe Clark, on the grounds that they have proven themselves incorrigible, throws them out of school. Once silence falls upon the auditorium he begins his first pep talk to the entire student body. He reminds them that the school is built upon a cemetery and that at the moment it is dead, but that ghosts are spirits that rise from the dead. He tells the students that they are going to lead his (Joe Clark's) resurrection (note again the religious overtones) by defying the expectations of all those who assume that a school such as Eastside High, in its present condition, is doomed to failure. He also tells the students that, should they fail, they can't blame their parents or their teachers. He reminds them that they are in school for the sole reason of learning, that they need to work for what they want, otherwise they'll never have a chance to participate in the American dream. And the alternative to taking charge and becoming responsible for themselves is to waste their time and "to fall into the trap of crime, drugs, and death." His final words, "Welcome to the new Eastside High," are met with hushed silence and an uncertain expression on most faces.

Of course the expulsion of the "hoodlums" and "drug dealers" meets with an instant political reaction. A meeting is called by a parental group where a certain Mrs. Barrett (whose son was among those expelled) becomes the spokesperson of the opposition to what Joe Clark has already undertaken. Joe Clark actually begins to use a kind of religious rhetoric here (to which Mrs. Barrett's first response is to remind him that they "are not in church"). In the eyes of some he may sound a bit blasphemous when he quotes Christ's words ("My God, my God, why hast thou forsaken me?"), but it should be noted (even if it's merely a coincidence) that his initials are the same as those of Jesus Christ. Be that as it may, his ploy of asserting that he has made a promise to God that he will do whatever it takes to help the young people in the school rise and that's why he "threw those bastards out," goes over well with most of those present. Most of the parents at this meeting applaud him. This is the first real sign that what he is attempting to do is seen by some at least as something necessary and worthwhile, his apparently intolerant egomaniacal non-compromising tyranny notwithstanding.

By now I think most viewers will be curious to see just how Joe Clark will manage to turn the school around and to raise those test scores to the 75 percent required by the state. Clashes will now follow clashes, but in each case some inkling of a positive reaction will emerge in spite of the apparently arrogant and intolerant (no nonsense, if you will) attitude of Joe Clark. First we will find him in an act I can only call "tough love," where Thomas Sams, one of the expelled students, comes to beg the principal to allow him to return to school. Joe Clark takes Thomas Sams to the roof and tells him that if he continues his drug use, he is slowly going to kill himself, so he might as well do the job quickly and jump off the roof right then and there. It should be clear to anyone that this tough love stance is an act, that Joe Clark is not mean-spirited, that he is using strong language because he really and truly wants to get through to the young man. When Thomas Sams is allowed to go back down, the camera stays with Joe Clark and we can clearly see a sigh, not of relief, but of the acknowledgement to himself that he certainly has his work cut out for him. One down and who knows how many more to go.

The scene in the cafeteria takes us further along to bits and pieces of evidence that some of the students are beginning to respond to him positively (the young woman, for example, who gets his okay to sign up for a class in auto mechanics). Joe Clark's apparent obsession with the school song also has a purpose (which may escape some for quite a while). It is simply symbolic, as it were, of an attempt on his part to make the students take ownership of their pride in their school. At this point, though, open clashes with some of the teachers emerge. The black English teacher who bends down to pick up a piece of paper is severely reprimanded for having moved during the performance of the school song. The music teacher, whose class Joe Clark interrupts during a rehearsal of a Mozart piece, is the first to sound a certain note of perhaps legitimate dissatisfaction with Joe Clark's ways: "If you would like us to respect your work, you could try to appreciate ours." Joe Clark, though, has no ear for this. He ends up firing the teacher (said to be one of the best in the school) for "insubordination." His next clash, in his office, is with the black English teacher who dared to move during the performance of the school song. He, too, sounds the same note of the need for mutual respect for which his reward is immediate suspension. The black English teacher leaves in anger, but not without turning Joe Clark's desk on its side. When

Ms. Levias, the vice principal, tells Joe Clark that he is causing chaos with his tyrannical rule, he remains unmoved.

While the students are taking a practice basic skills test, the background song says, among other things, "forget diplomas, it's education I hate." There is more to this than meets the eye (or, in this case, the ear). They don't (as will emerge in the rest of the story) "hate" education at all. What they hate is the chaos that reigns in school, the chaos that makes learning impossible while relegating it to a place of no respect in the face of all the apparently uncontrollable misbehavior. Joe Clark was right when he first stated that if you can't control the school, you can't teach. Already, though, there are more and more signs of positive responses from the students. But the "battle" has hardly begun. A drug dealer who has been expelled comes back and starts a fight with another student (also, apparently, involved with drugs). Joe Clark intervenes and when the expelled student pulls a switchblade on him, he hits the student in the head with his bullhorn. This is the scene that leads to the chains and locks on the door, which in turn leads to the clash between politics and education and, in a way, between the letter and the spirit of the law.

In the meantime we get more evidence of the fact that, contrary to popular opinion, Joe Clark has a heart. When he learns that Kaneesha's mother no longer wants her around, he and the vice principal pay her a visit and talk her out of putting Kaneesha in a foster home. This is a sad inner-city story, of course, but this, too, is an indication that no matter how hopeless things may seen, they are not necessarily permanent. But now the chains-on-doors controversy irrupts. The first person to reprimand Joe Clark is his old friend, Frank Napier, the Superintendent of Schools. Joe Clark states that those who are worried about the chains don't have a "personal stake" at what goes on in the school. Frank Napier is angry, though, and tells Joe that he is "screwing up," that he is "alienating everybody," that he is "plain loco." When Joe Clark mentions that they are "being crucified by a process" that's turning students into a "permanent underclass," we can once more hear the religious overtones that crop up from time to time. At this point, though, Frank Napier feels that Joe's "personal battles" may cost them "the war." Once more the note of the need for mutual respect is sounded when Frank tells Joe that if he is "so hot on discipline, then" he should "start by accepting" his. Joe Clark is to apologize to certain people he has offended and he is to reinstate the black English teacher he has suspended.

By the time the fire chief first strikes, as it were, and is turned away from the school, we also see that more and more of the students approve of what Joe Clark is doing. In fact, some of the teachers are clearly behind him as well. I love the exchange, for example, between Mr. Darnell (the black English teacher) and Joe Clark when the former says "you shouldn't have fired me in the first place," and the latter remarks, "you are right, but don't get used to it." The smile on Mr. Darnell's face tells us a great deal. The chains-on-the-door issue, though, is another clear instance of politics vs. education. The chains on doors could, of course, be devastating in case of a fire (which is why they are illegal), but at the same time (and the students as well as the teachers recognize this, too) they have made it possible for peace to return to the school, the kind of peace that's conducive to learning. The students are clearly doing positive things by now, too, that they haven't done before. When it becomes apparent, for example, that someone has taught them a jazzed-up version of the school song, Joe Clark confronts Mrs. Powers with her "unauthorized" intervention, only to heap praises on her. A sign that Joe Clark is, after all, capable of appreciating the work of others.

But things are, unfortunately, still not where they should be. When the practice test scores come back and are still woefully inadequate, Joe Clark reprimands the entire faculty on the grounds that they are not doing their job. Still the preparations for the real test are by now underway in a changed atmosphere. The decorations going up in the hallways, the reminders of the number of days till the test, the words of the background song played at this point ("everybody needs somebody") all indicate that teamwork has taken over, that there is a kind of enthusiasm operative at Eastside High the school probably hasn't seen in a long, long time. At the same time the plot against Joe Clark over the chains on the door is thickening. Mrs. Barrett is the leader of this plot, though the fire chief and the mayor are not far behind. While the concern is a legally legitimate one, Mrs. Barrett's motives are clearly not innocent. When the mayor says that she would like to see Joe Clark's "head on a platter," once more we are given that bit of religious rhetoric that rears its head in the movie from time to time. Mrs. Barrett is after blood, though, to the point of threatening the mayor by promising to work against his reelection. The mayor strikes a deal with her. The plan is to let Joe Clark administer the basic skills test and then to let Mrs. Barrett, who is to be appointed to the School Board, get rid of him, provided that they can catch Eastside High with the chains on the door (which will be up to the fire chief to do). Luckily for Joe Clark, the school lawyer overhears the plot (in the men's room, of all places) and warns him. By now the teachers are clearly on his side, too, as they all agree to try to prevent the authorities from catching the school in the act of having the doors chained and locked.

By this time it is also clear that the students are coming to Joe Clark more and more as if he were their father rather than the "crazy" and stern principal according to his reputation. Yet it is at this point that Ms. Levias approaches him in the corridor in order to ask for a transfer. Their exchange is going to convert, as it were, Joe Clark. Ms. Levias tells him in no uncertain terms that he is not alone in the fight they have all undertaken to turn the school around, that the teachers care just as much about everything as he does, yet for him it is all "I, I, I, I." That he won't listen, that he is "thoughtless, cruel," and that it "hurts." It is not until the next assembly (after Joe Clark has put into Ms. Levias's hands the envelope containing the transfer papers she has previously requested) that Joe Clark shows himself a changed man. He acknowledges that they, teachers and students alike, are all in this together. And he thanks a "dear friend" for having pointed this out to him (at which point he is directly looking at Ms. Levias standing not far from the stage in the packed auditorium).

This scene is a major turning point in the life of Eastside High. In his speech Joe Clark tells the students that there are those "out there" who think they are inferior and incapable of learning. He tells them that they are not. He whips them into a frenzy of enthusiasm for the upcoming basic skills test by telling them (without mincing his words) that the students should make "liars out of those bastards." He reminds them that they are all in possession of a "spirit that will not die." This assembly culminates in Mrs. Powers leading the entire student body, together with the teachers, in singing the song "Lean On Me." The students and teachers are clearly of one mind, in perfect harmony. And we watch with joy Ms. Levias crumple the envelope containing her transfer papers. While the students are taking the basic skills test, though, Mrs. Barrett demands action. She manages to get a court order to get past the guards at Eastside High. The fire chief strikes. The "enemy" gets within the gates. Joe Clark's remark to call for "Code 10" is captured on tape. He is arrested and hauled off to jail. It is clear that neither the students nor the teachers are happy with this, to say the least. While Joe Clark is waiting in his jail cell, the School Board is meeting, in the presence of the mayor, the superintendent of schools, and the school's lawyer. Mrs. Barrett's ploy is now to insist that Joe Clark has failed (she bases it on the low scores the students received on the practice basic skills test) and that (before the scores for the real test come in) they should fire him and replace him with someone else. It is clear from her stance that she is interested in one thing and one thing only, to get rid of Joe Clark, ultimately as a political act of personal vendetta.

Frank Napier, though, is not having any of this. He comes to see Joe Clark in his jail cell and tells him that he has no complaints, that "those kids have a light in their eyes" they may have never had before and that it's all thanks to Joe Clark. As we watch Joe Clark lie comfortably on his cot in his jail cell, we hear shouting in the distance. It soon becomes clear that the entire student body is coming to protest. They are chanting "Free Mr. Clark, Free Mr. Clark." The meeting of the School Board turns into a pandemonium. The mayor comes to see Joe Clark to appeal to him to talk the student body into dispersing. Mrs. Barrett goes out to the top of the stairs and tries to address the students. She speaks of Joe Clark having broken the law, but one student responds by saying that she is twisting the law, that what Joe Clark did was good for the school, that he is more than a principal, that he is a father most of the students have never had. This outpouring of love and affection is irrepressible, and when Ms. Levias arrives with the test scores, Joe Clark's triumph is unmistakable. He announces with pleasure that the students of Eastside High have passed the state's exam and that the mayor can, therefore, "tell the state to go to hell." The students cheer and burst into the school song.

Almost all of the reviews I have seen of this movie express a dislike for Joe Clark's methods. They acknowledge that what he accomplishes is something good, but they still can't seem to accept his methods. They overlook the fact that the movie is not advocating this method as a general rule, only under dire circumstances, where nothing else seems to be working. The fact that such circumstances may prevail at many an inner-city school is precisely what should give us pause. What the movie is saying is that there may be times when there is no substitute for personal involvement by a strong and caring and capable leader. The cumulative effect of all the things that Joe Clark has given voice to from time to time is that, indeed, you cannot teach if you have no control over the school, that learning requires a tranquil and peaceful environment, that teachers must be dedicated to the proposition of doing their utmost to awaken enthusiasm for learning in their students and, finally, that we are all in this together. This is the essence of what this movie is trying to say. It does not go into details of the nitty-gritty of teaching, of what actually goes on in the classroom. We are to take it on faith that once the environment has been cleaned up, that once the enthusiasm of the teachers and the students has been awakened, real teaching and real learning could finally take place. The proof of the pudding is in the final test scores.

Politics has no business in teaching. Except to the degree to which it might aid and abet it. And teachers should be free to ply their trade as best as they see fit. Only in an atmosphere of freedom, freedom from external as well as internal interference, can both teachers and students realize their full potential. If at times it takes the monomaniacal personal commitment of a Joe Clark to achieve this goal, so be it. There are times when only a true leader, selflessly dedicated to the cause, can turn things around. Would that this happened more often in life, too, than it, in fact, does.

4. Oleanna

[Movie Log: Released in 1994 by The Samuel Goldwyn Company in association with Channel Four Films. Screenplay by David Mamet, based on his own play. Directed by David Mamet. Cast: Debra Eisenstadt (Carol); William H. Macy (John)]

> *The printed text of the play begins with a folk song that refers to "Oleanna," the name of a utopian community in Norway that failed to flourish because its inhabitants could not (or did not) live up to their high ideals. The word "Oleanna" then came to signify a fallen Eden.*
>
> —Note to play in *Responding to Literature*

I shall begin with a free paraphrase of an interesting remark made by Roland Barthes, the famous French critic: the person who never sees the same movie twice is destined to watch the same movie over and over again (the English translation of the original of this insight is "those who fail to reread are obliged to read the same story everywhere"). Let me continue with first impressions, then, or how it may strike an innocent eye:

27

I will resort to a little trick here and share with you my own first impressions of this movie as it is recorded in an e-mail I sent to a friend a few days after I first saw *Oleanna*. The e-mail is dated January 13, 1996. It reads as follows: It was last Wednesday evening, prime time, and I was looking for a movie to watch. The title *Oleanna* caught my attention, so I checked in the *TV Guide* for more details. This is what I found: "*Oleanna* (1994) NR: Adult themes. David Mamet wrote and directed this two-character psychological study about a sexual harassment charge leveled against a professor (William H. Macy) by a failing student (Debra Eisenstadt)."

I expected a straightforward story about a female student who (unjustly, as I anticipated) would for some reason bring charges against a professor for sexual harassment. As I began to watch the movie, though, I was almost immediately disturbed. The professor seemed rude to the student in his office (unrealistically gorgeous and ornate, but let that go). He is preoccupied. He is on the phone, obviously talking to his wife about buying a house and some sort of glitch with the realtor (or seller). The student seems unduly assertive about her "dumbness." She says things like "I don't get it," "I don't understand anything," but says this in an accusatory tone, as if the professor were to be blamed for her own lack of understanding. And I said, "What the hell is going on here?" I was practically ready to switch to another channel, but I stayed with the movie, though my irritation kept rising. Here's a rude professor with a student rather militantly aggressive in her ignorance, I thought. I just didn't like any of this, but I kept on watching.

Then there is a twist in the plot. The student's need for attention wins the professor over from his preoccupation with buying the house and with getting his tenure. Suddenly he sees the young woman as she "really" is, a student with low self-esteem and performance anxiety (as when taking tests, for example). He is suddenly kind to her. Tells her about his own prior problems with self-esteem, how he was constantly told that he was "stupid" when he was young, until he began to believe it. He tries to have the young woman rethink her own situation. At this point I thought "Oh well, so this is what the story is all about."

It is at this point that the professor offers to cancel the young woman's failing grade and tells her that at the moment she has an "A" in the course. He tells her that he is willing to help her earn the high grade with, as it were, private tutoring sessions in his office. "Oh well," I thought, "I am beginning to see what this is really all about. The teacher who is preoccupied with other things has to stop worrying about his (or her) own concerns and concentrate on those of his (or her) students. Good point," I thought. But soon (and I can't pinpoint the exact moment) I realized that none of this had anything to do with what the movie is really about. My final readjustment came about half-way through the movie when it dawned on me that we are up against a sort of allegory here about political correctness, the standard attack on the "white European male" who is seen as the "fascist" or "Nazi" oppressor of women and none-whites (and the destroyer of nature to boot).

By halfway through the movie (or so) it becomes apparent that the young woman is not some "dumb" student. In fact, she is a sort of feminist agent, working for some feminist group. Her presence in the professor's office is a calculated challenge to his authority. At this point in the story interesting arguments surface. She says things like "Who the hell do you think you are that you can just write your own agenda, indulge yourself with your own theories, ideas, challenge higher education," etc. "Students come to you to learn, not to listen to your own pet peeves." Good points, I thought, though I was somewhat disturbed because what she was saying would interfere with the professor's academic freedom to teach as he sees fit (it's only in totalitarian societies, whether fascist or communist or fundamentalistically religious makes no difference, that teachers are told what and how to teach. Let me add that I have, in fact, been thinking of late that political correctness carried to extremes is a new kind of McCarthyism, not at all subtle and rather insidious).

But then things really turn vicious. The student accuses the professor of sexual harassment. Not directly, as it were. What she says is that certain things he has previously said or done might be so construed, as when he offered her an "A" and told her to come to his office for private lessons— of course, it's clear to the viewer that this was an honest offer, and this seems also clear to the student who nevertheless makes the point that the accusation would be possible, according to the strict letter of law, and would probably hold up in court. By this time she even admits to be the spokesperson for a "group." Finally, what I have referred to above as a kind of McCarthyism really becomes apparent. It appears that the student has sent a petition to the tenure committee, asking them to deny the professor tenure (on sexual harassment grounds, among other things). The movie finally erupts in violence. When the young woman brazenly tells him not to call his wife "baby" (he has just been talking to her on the phone again), the professor loses it, turns on the young woman and physically (not sexually) assaults her (he even mentions political correctness as he does this). In the final scene the professor is sitting on a chair he was just about to hurl at the young woman, saying "Oh my God, oh my God," while the young woman is crouching in fear a few feet from him saying "oh yes," or something like that, I don't recall her exact words.

There are moments in the movie when the hostility between the young woman and the middle-aged man is almost overcome with understanding and tenderness, but understanding and tenderness don't have a chance in the face of the ideologically-charged atmosphere which otherwise permeates the world inhabited by the two characters. I remember thinking that "Oleanna" is something like "Pollyanna" but with a huge difference. The word reminds me of "oleander," which is a poisonous plant. The movie isn't subtle (perhaps because it "allegorizes" its theme too obviously) but it is clearly against this poisonously politically correct atmosphere that would, if it could, throw the baby out with the proverbial bathwater. In any case, this movie was a challenge to watch. I suddenly found myself having to practice what I usually preach about good reading: don't let your own prior prejudices get in the way and don't jump to premature conclusions. While watching the movie I was conscious of having to readjust my expectations several times. I wish I could tape it and study it some more.

Thus ends the e-mail representing my first impressions. Since then I have learned more about this movie and have learned to view it both as a critique of political correctness as well as perhaps to some extent also a critique of what political correctness is a reaction against. The stakes are high, but the choice is not quite as difficult or impossible as certain quarters might make it out to be. In a crude first reaction women (particularly those with a feminist bent) may side with the student in the story, while men (not necessarily those with a conservative bent) may side with the professor. The tagline to the movie states that it doesn't matter which side you take, you are going to be wrong. This implies that equal weight is given to the two sides. Let's call the first (that represented by the "feminist" student) the politically correct side and let's call the second (that represented by the professor) the traditional side. (Of course the politically correct side is bound to call the traditional side patriarchal and sexist and elitist, but let's wait before making judgments on these issues).

This is a highly text-oriented movie. More emphasis is placed here on the spoken word (and on the arguments that evolve) than is usual and customary. One can almost call this movie a filmed stage play (which, in a real sense, it is, though the action added to the stage play is minimal, but in a few instances rather telling). Without repeating much of what I have already said in my e-mail quoted above, I am now going to proceed with the benefit of several viewings of the movie as well as of having read the text of the play. As I just indicated, what is said here is of paramount importance if we are going to see that the movie, in fact, probably comes down on the side of "tradition" as against the emerging political correctness (which, if push really came to shove, would destroy education as we know it). I think a careful weighing of the (verbal) evidence in the story logically leads to this conclusion (and I mention this here so as to be upfront about the argument I am claiming the movie itself is making).

From the beginning Carol and John seem to speak at cross-purposes a lot. Since John is preoccupied, it takes him a little time to adjust, as it were, and really pay attention to Carol's alleged problem (her alleged difficulties with John's course). He quickly gets "personal" in a positive way. His motive is clearly to help Carol get rid of her low self-esteem. And he even mentions the fact that he wishes someone had talked to him in this "personal" way when he was a student. He uses words here and there that will backfire on him (and when we first see the movie we don't even suspect that his words could possibly be misconstrued in the way in which the politically correct interpretation is going to misconstrue them). John suggests that they remove "the artificial stricture of Teacher and Student" (the idea is to just talk to each other as two well-meaning human beings ought to talk to each other). He mentions the built-in "idiocy" of tests and indicates that even he faces this sort of thing with respect to the Tenure Committee. It is at this point, too, that John offers Carol a grade of "A" for the course. What he means is quite clear. Carol is worried about her grade. So he offers her the "A" with the chance to earn it. And he even offers to help her, in a series of visits to his office (in a kind of private tutoring way). This offer is also going to be misconstrued by the politically correct "group" (and already we might pay attention to how innocent words and gestures can be seen in a negative albeit uncalled-for light).

At this point we even get a sampling of how and just what Carol could possibly learn in these office visits and also how she might thus earn the grade of "A." It seems that John has been making challenging remarks about the usefulness of higher education in class. He now explains to Carol what he meant by these (and also explains the significance of the "hazing" metaphor). He tells Carol that we have come to think of higher education for everyone as a kind of automatic entitlement without stopping to think what it should really be for and whether or not it equally benefits everyone. We have, John states, a "predilection"—if you will—a "prejudice" in favor of higher education to such an extent that if someone questions it, we become "angry." This is an excellent point, but a point that Carol is apparently not capable of understanding (again, as it will be evident, she will have understood it quite well but will have vehemently disagreed with it on account of her heavy politically correct ideology).

At this point some very ambiguous exchanges occur (which are, again, ambiguous on account of the still at this point unknown agency of political correctness). John tells Carol that his job is to provoke her (meaning, to provoke her into questioning and thinking for herself), to make her "mad." Again he gets personal in a way that will severely backfire on him. He uses a sexually charged metaphor (in a way) when he indicates that someone once gave him a criterion by which he kept judging things that had nothing to do with anything. (These are the "offending" words John uses: "When I was young somebody told me, are you ready, [that] the rich copulate less often than the poor. But when they do, they take more of their clothes off.") It is shortly after this anecdote (clearly a kind of innocent joke) that John, in a paternal gesture, puts his arms on Carol's shoulders, which she clearly misconstrues because she quickly walks away from him. And at this point a very intriguing moment occurs. One of those moments I had earlier referred to as perhaps moments of understanding and tenderness. Carol suddenly accuses herself of being "bad," and she is about to confess something she says she has "never told anyone" before. But (as it happens a number of times in the movie) the phone rings, the moment is ruined, and we never do find out what Carol was about to confide to John.

By the next scene the cat is out of the bag. It becomes apparent that Carol has been playing the fool, that her low self-esteem has just been an act, that she is really (in a sense) a spy in the house of learning, a kind of *agent provocateur*. It appears that Carol has filed a complaint with the Tenure Committee in which she has charged John with sexism and elitism and a tendency to waste the class's time "in non-prescribed, in self-aggrandizing and theatrical diversions from the prescribed text" and "that these have taken both sexist and pornographic forms." In this report the earlier remark about the sex lives of the rich vs. the poor becomes "a rambling, sexually explicit story, in which frequency and attitudes of fornication of the poor and the rich are, it would seem, the central point." The report also includes a mention of John's having laid his hands on Carol's shoulders, but now this is seen as an "embrace," all "part of a pattern" of "sexist misconduct" (which will be the first item on a list of "charges" against the professor made into a poster—this is, by the way, not in the play, just in the movie).

John's first reaction is to call the whole thing "ludicrous" (which it clearly is—as viewers we have seen the interaction between the two and can clearly see that indeed the charges are grossly exaggerated and, in fact, misconstrued). But now a significant shift of power occurs. It is suddenly Carol who has nothing to lose, who has come to "teach" John about his own "vile" ways. When John uses the expression "Good men and true" with respect to the Tenure Committee, Carol's reaction is to mention the fact that since one member of the committee is a woman, this "traditional" expression (no matter how innocent the intention in using it) is sexist, in fact, "pornographic," sufficiently so to deprive John of his tenure. It seems that in Carol's politically correct eyes no professor has a right to teach as he sees fit. Earlier John had said that he never wanted to be a "rigid automaton" as an "instructor," but it seems that in the eyes of the politically correct that's all any teacher is ever allowed to be, not a person but a teaching machine, one who has no *persona*, no personality, one who is (in a fact) not allowed to be a human being at all. One who simply follows prescribed rules and procedures and never deviates from them, never adding anything of him or herself to the process of teaching.

In spite of all this John is still belaboring under the illusion that he can level with Carol, that they can settle their differences as two human beings, pure and simple. But Carol now wants to "stick to the process." And when she attempts to leave, and John (out of desperation, as he feels he has more to say) physically restrains her (though only for a few seconds and not with force), Carol tears herself away from him rather violently and even shouts for "help" as she exists John's office where people in the corridor can hear her and see the tail end of the commotion. As the scene ends, the camera stays with John's bewildered face. It's as if he knew that the situation has by now gotten completely out of hand and that his "goose is" now definitely "cooked."

The next time she comes to his office (at John's request) Carol won't even "allow" him to call the accusations leveled at him "alleged." She says that "evidence" has been presented to John's "superiors" who have found him "negligent" and "guilty" and "wanting" and "in error," and thus nothing is "alleged" here, everything is "proved." There has been no trial, of course, John has not been as yet given an official chance to answer the charges, but it seems that for the politically correct the American principle of "innocent before proven guilty" has no longer any relevance whatsoever. Carol's next speech is quite clear on what is really at stake here now. When John objects that he has done nothing that should warrant the loss of his job (and we should keep in mind that tenure is not just security against getting fired but that its original intention was to protect a professor's "academic freedom," so that those who disagreed with him or her could not fire him or her just because of such disagreements, provided—of course—that the professor in question remained within the legitimate parameters of his or her field), Carol clearly indicates that none of this matters any more:

> You don't understand? You're angry? What has led you to this place? Not your sex. Not your race. Not your class. Your own actions! And you're angry. You ask me here. What do you want? You want to "charm" me. You want to "convince" me. You want me to recant. I will *not* recant. Why should I? What I say is right. You tell me, you are going to tell me that you have a wife and child. You are going to say that you have a career and that you have worked for twenty years for this. Do you know what you have worked for? Power! For power! Do you understand? And you sit there and tell me stories. About your house, about all the private schools, and about privilege, and how you are entitled. To buy, to spend, to mock, to summon... Don't you see? You worked twenty years for the right to insult me! And you feel entitled to be paid for it.

In other words, the verdict is in. There is nothing John can do to save himself. Carol tells him, twice, that he is not God. And she has nothing to gain from him, though he may still have something to gain from her. Once he admits that he "hates" her by this point (on account of the power *she* and her "group" have over him), Carol makes it clear that what is happening to him is a version of "what goes around comes around." Just as students can be at the mercy of professors, in these changed times professors will be at the mercy of students. Not quite. Rather, it seems that they will be at the mercy of a merciless and perhaps mindless and completely inhumane and "mechanical" political correctness. Carol also accuses him of not really believing in freedom of thought except as long as it is part of "an elitist" and "protected hierarchy" which "rewards" the likes of him.

There is by now another layer of significance operating here that the viewer may not be able to detect when watching the movie for the first time. John is, almost until the very end, unaware of the fact that charges of attempted rape are also possible against him and that Carol has in fact been seeing a lawyer about this. So it's not just his "job" that's at stake. When Carol mentions "physical caress" and John's rejoinder is that "it was devoid of sexual content," his intentions are again for naught. "I say it was not," says Carol, twice. "It's not for you to say." Yet in all this Carol insists that she doesn't want "revenge," that all she wants is "understanding." By this time the two are at cross-purposes even more than has ever been the case up to this point. When John says that his "job" is lost now, Carol offers him a way of saving it. As it turns out, the offer would mean that John would be simply putty in the hands of the politically correct powers-that-be. His book, for example, would be "banned." All his freedom to teach as he sees fit would be taken away from him.

John finds this "compromise" unacceptable. It's not until he gets another phone call that it dawns on him that attempted rape might also be leveled at him. What is very important to keep in mind here is that even Carol knows that this is based on a mere technicality, a legal maneuver, a strict application of the letter of the law. This is in reference to the last time Carol was leaving John's office. Indeed for a split second he "pressed" his body against hers, but clearly his intention was to restrain her from leaving just yet. Even Carol knows that this can only be construed as an "attempted rape" "under the statute." What finally takes John to the point of no return, to the point of violence, is the proverbial straw that can even break the camel's back. When he is on the phone for the last time, with his wife, he calls her "baby." When Carol reprimands him for this "sexist" behavior, John can take it no longer. He hits her, several times, quite violently. I am not sure I hear the words "political correctness" in the movie. And perhaps it's not even necessary to spell this out in the end. I think we can all recognize it anyway, from fairly early on. In any case, the words are used in the play. When John finally physically assaults Carol, he does this with the words: "You vicious little bitch. You think you can come here with your political correctness and destroy my life?"

What he does, of course, is not to be condoned. The ending is inconclusive. We leave them there in John's office, Carol is cowering on the floor, and John is saying "Oh my God, oh my God," while sitting down in the chair he has just about hurled at Carol a second before. Her last words "that's right" don't amount to any definitive conclusion. The movie doesn't tell us how to pass final judgment on the whole course of events that have just transpired before our eyes and have ended in a kind of tragedy, a tragedy that perhaps awaits higher education itself. I am sure that the movie exaggerates. I read it as an allegory of sorts. A clash in the culture wars we have been hearing about for a while now. It's one thing to recognize that times have changed, that professors can no longer give themselves the luxury to engage in certain kinds of banter, but it's quite another to throw the proverbial baby out with the bathwater. Any extreme ideology can undermine freedom of thought, freedom of inquiry. If we don't permit those to speak with whose views we don't agree, than we are no better than any totalitarian regime. The minute you have to toe the party line or else, education has been replaced by indoctrination. According to its etymology, "education" means an "out-leading." And the word "liberal" in the traditional liberal arts is there to indicate that the purpose of an education is to liberate the students from the prejudices of their time and place. According to a classical dictum the unexamined life is not worth living. Neither are unexamined ideas worth holding. If they are true, questioning won't hurt them. But if they are false (yet believed), we should be able to change our minds about them. Teaching is an art. As such it requires the kind of freedom the artist needs, the kind of creative control, say, David Mamet has himself exercised when writing and directing the movie itself. No, the movie doesn't tell us what to think, but it (like all good education) shows us what is at stake in the clash between, for lack of better words, the politically correct and the traditionally not always perfect but at least free to change and to improve as necessary. The movie doesn't tell us what judgment to pass here, but it does provide the evidence necessary to make the right judgment, the judgment that should save education from becoming little more than a rigidly administered indoctrination.

Chapter Two
Hollywood Falls in Love

1. The Age of Innocence

[Movie Log: Released by Columbia Pictures in 1993. Screenplay by Martin Scorsese and Jay Cocks, based on the Edith Wharton novel. Directed by Martin Scorsese. Cast: Daniel Day-Louis (Newland Archer); Michelle Pfeiffer (Ellen Olenska); Winona Ryder (May Welland); Miriam Margolyes (Mrs. Mingott); Geraldine Chaplin (Mrs. Welland); Siân Phillips (Mrs. Archer); Stuart Wilson (Julius Beaufort); Michael Gough (Henry van der Luyden); Alec McGowen (Sillerton Jackson); Richard E. Grant (Larry Lefferts)]

> *Ah, no, he [Newland] did not want May to have that kind of innocence, the innocence that seals the mind against imagination and the heart against experience!*
> —Edith Wharton, *The Age of Innocence*

Although very faithful to the novel, the movie never does give us the significance that "innocence" carries in the title. It is not something good and desirable, it is more like a kind of denial rooted in ignorance (the etymological meaning of innocence) of all that's beyond the pale of our immediate circle, our own close-knit and unbending society. The tagline for the movie uses the word in its more ordinary sense: "In a world of tradition, in an age of innocence, they dared to break the rules."

This is a love story set against the rigid societal backdrop of the New York of the 1870s. Here conformity rules. And the desires of the individual must be sacrificed upon the altar of the most rigidly controlled external forms of behavior. The beginning is a miniature "allegory" of the whole: we are in the opera where Larry Lefferts and Sillerton Jackson check out and criticize Madame Olenska as she enters the Mingott's box. Newland Archer overhears their disapproving words and immediately leaves to walk over to the box where May Welland, his fiancée is sitting in the company of her mother, Mrs. Welland, and Madame Olenska, newly returned from Europe where she has been living in a bad marriage. It is Newland's attempt to stand by Ellen Olenska that figures as the miniature "allegory" of the whole story. Disapproval of the unconventional reigns supreme in this world, and those who dare defy the customs of the tribe may have hell to pay.

From the very beginning Newland's "desire" to marry May is caught up in his response to Ellen and her trials and tribulations. He wants Ellen to know that he and May (Ellen is May's cousin) are engaged, and he wants to announce their engagement later in the same evening, at the Beaufort ball, in order to have two families stand behind Ellen Olenska against the disapproval of the close-knit society of the New York of the 1870s. May's immediate response to this suggestion is to ask why they should "change what is already settled?" And in this world everything seems "already settled," so it's with a certain amount of irony that we may see Ellen's feeling that she has come to a place very much like "heaven," to an America that she associates with freedom. The reality belies this assumption with a vengeance. When on the next day Ellen arrives at the Mignott house in the company of Julius Beaufort, who simply ran into her and decided to walk her home, Mrs. Welland remarks that it is a "mistake for Ellen to be seen parading up Fifth Avenue with Julius Beaufort at the crowded hour."

At the dinner table in the Archer house the criticisms continue. And Newland, as will be his wont, comes to Ellen's rescue by declaring, in no uncertain terms, that Ellen's unhappy situation is not her fault and that it shouldn't make her an outcast. When later Sillerton Jackson recites further rumors about the secretary who helped Ellen get away from her husband, Newland once more comes to her defense. To Jackson's question whether a "woman should have the same freedom as a man," Newland's response is a resounding "yes." Newland gives the impression of being a rather freethinking person, a potential rebel, if you will, in a society entirely organized around rigid conventions.

The conflict throughout the movie is between the espousal of inherited ideas and the attempt to divorce oneself from them. Newland Archer walks a fine line between these alternatives, yet (as the story progresses) he is tempted by both the freedom offered to him by Ellen Olenska (a freedom that would bring with it the ruination of their reputation in the world in which they live) and by the peace and quiet imposed upon him by following the rules of total conformity. The first alternative would offer

39

him a world of passion, the second the world of a dull and routine existence. The peace of marital bliss is not necessarily the kind that passes understanding.

When to the horror of the Mignott clan all those invited to a formal dinner to meet the Countess Olenska decline, the Archers appeal to the highest-ranking family in New York, the van der Luydens, to come to their rescue. Newland's theory for the snub (a "total eradication" of Ellen Olenska) is itself indicative of a hypocritical undercurrent in the smooth operation of the New York of the story. He thinks that Larry Lefferts is behind it in order to make himself look moral, probably because he has been involved in some extra-marital shenanigans for which his moral outrage would be a cover-up. Whether this is so or not is neither here nor there.

It is at the van der Luyden party, given in honor of their cousin, the Duke of St. Austrey, that Newland begins to respond to the freedom embodied by the Countess Olenska. She arrives late but without the slightest degree of compunction over the fact. Then she breaks another rule when she leaves the Duke and comes over to sit with Newland for a chat. It is ironic, of course, that Ellen thinks of New York as a place where "nothing has to be traditional." She thinks of the "blind obeying of tradition" as "thoroughly needless." This is theoretically true of America, but in reality nothing could be further from what is actually going on. When Ellen suggests that the proposed marriage between Newland and May is a "true romance," which is "not in the least arranged," Newland actually reprimands her by reminding her of the fact that in America "we don't allow marriages to be arranged."

Again, this is of course theoretically true, but in a far more subtle way the proposed marriage between Newland and May couldn't have been more arranged than if their respective parents had entered the young couple into it without even consulting them. The whole society of the upper-crust New York of their world is firmly behind this union and it won't brook any suggestion to an alternative, a truly self-imposed arrangement (as would be the case if Ellen divorced her husband and married Newland—that would be an unarranged marriage but one that the society in question would never tolerate and would use its utmost power to prevent from coming into being). Which is actually the remainder of the whole story. Yet how it unfolds is layered with deeper significance and even deeper ironies.

The first irony is Newland's nonsensical jealousy of Julius Beaufort, a married man with an ambiguous reputation but of great commercial success whose business practices are behind many of the members of the circle of families tied together into the world of the New York of the 1870s. Every time Ellen shows up with Beaufort, Newland is a bit irritated. He sees himself in a kind of rivalry with Beaufort for Ellen's affection, failing to realize that Ellen's relations with him are strictly easy-going and all "business."

So this rivalry (although it will have a devastatingly negative effect on any possible union between Newland and Ellen) is simply a figment of Newland's imagination.

The attraction between Ellen and Newland is there almost from the very beginning, but it is not clear just how conscious of it they themselves may at first be. In any case, Ellen invites Newland to come and see her twice before his first visit to her house. When he arrives Ellen is out, so he has a chance to look around her place, where he finds paintings more modern and daring than those in most of the New York households of the time. When Ellen returns, it is in the company of Julius Beaufort, who has—as Ellen explains to Newland—taken her to see some houses, as her present place of residence may not be regarded as suitable to a person in her station in life. It is actually respectable enough but perhaps not suitably fashionable. To Ellen's question about the importance of being fashionable Newland's response is that fashion is a serious consideration to all those "who have nothing more serious to consider."

There is something slightly sinister in this remark, as it points to a world in which trivial considerations are of paramount importance while what should be important has to be sugar-coated with the semblance of respectability. When a little later Newland reminds Ellen that "all the older women like and admire her," she responds by saying, "Oh, I know, I know. But only if they don't hear anything unpleasant. Does no one here want to know the truth, Mr. Archer? The real loneliness is living among all these kind people who only ask you to pretend." It is here, in a moment of deeply felt compassion, that Newland first calls Ellen by her first name. And a little later, on an impulse, he sends her a bouquet of "yellow roses" but without including his card. She will nevertheless know that the roses came from him.

The family is now ready to impose its will on Ellen who is bent on divorcing her husband in order to regain her freedom. Newland is

41

recruited by the law firm he works for to intervene on the family's behalf. He is willing to do his bit in talking Ellen out of getting a divorce but only if she agrees. When he arrives at her house, he once more finds Julius Beaufort there, to his annoyance. Once they are alone, Newland tells Ellen that although the "legislation favors divorce," the "social customs" do not. Not, at any rate, "if the woman has appearances in the least degree against her, has exposed herself to any unconventional behavior to—to offensive insinuations." At this point Newland, in his zeal to help Ellen, is actually beginning to work against any possibility of an unconventional union between them (and at this point their attraction for each other is still perhaps in its infancy). He manages to persuade her to stop the divorce proceedings by intimating that it wouldn't be fair of him not to make her see how her family and friends "judge such matters."

The next night at the theater Newland is deeply moved by a play in which there is something reminiscent of his own renunciation of forbidden love. He wants to see Ellen but he gets no reply to his note asking for her permission to call. Days later he gets a note from her telling him that she "ran away the day after" she saw him at the play. It is when he joins her in the country that a ruinous misunderstanding will precipitate events that will separate them and hasten Newland's marriage to May. Alone in a house in the country their heretofore unconfessed love is ready to emerge. Newland wants to know what it is that she has been running away from (perhaps he hopes that she has been running away from him—which is the case), but when Julius Beaufort is seen approaching the building, Newland assumes, quite erroneously, that she has been running away from him. Ellen notices this misunderstanding but can't at the moment explain herself. Soon thereafter she sends Newland a note in which she implores him to let her explain something, but Newland has by now acted impulsively and has gone to see May in St. Augustine, where she is temporarily staying with her mother. Newland's purpose is to talk May into moving up the date of their marriage. May senses that something is amiss and actually gives Newland a way out by suggesting that if there is another woman in his life, it would be unacceptable to her to buy her happiness at the expense of, at the unhappiness of another (though this is in actuality what she will eventually do).

Earlier I have spoken (though not in these precise words) of a "something far more deeply interfused" (Wordsworth) going on in this story than the usual and customary conflict between passionate love and marriage. The next time Newland sees Ellen, he tells her of May's "offer" to let him off the hook. Here the two (Newland and Ellen) talk at cross-purposes for a while. Is there another woman? Does she love Newland? There is no other woman, says Newland in anger, but then he admits the truth by noting that May herself guessed it, though she was mistaken as to the identity of the other woman.

Here things take a radical turn in a perhaps unexpected direction. When Newland tells Ellen that she is the one he "would have married if it had been possible," her response is to indicate that it was he who has made it impossible by talking her out of the divorce. To Newland's insistence that nothing has as yet been done that cannot be undone a whole new consideration enters the picture. Ellen now admits that she has been given a different view of things, a view not ordinarily entertained by most people: they can't buy happiness at the expense of someone else's unhappiness. This is the same consideration that May herself has raised when she suggested that perhaps Newland is in love with another woman, but Ellen's position is more telling and, in a way, much more certainly unselfish and self-abnegating, something akin to a religious conversion. As she herself puts the case:

> Newland. You couldn't be happy if it meant being cruel. If we act any other way I'll be making you act against what I love in you most. And I can't go back to that way of thinking. Don't you see? I cannot love you unless I give you up.

This ends the first part of the story. Will Newland and Ellen's self-sacrifice work? Can it withstand the pressures of the passion that has been kindled in their heart of hearts? Everything seems to work out just fine. Newland and May get married and go to Europe for their honeymoon, but already something almost sinister surfaces there. When Newland suggests that they invite a certain Frenchman to dinner, May demurs on the grounds that the person in question is "common." Newland quietly resigns himself to this judgment and, as the narrator remarks: "With a chill he knew that, in future, many problems would be solved for him in the same way." In the same way in which Newland seems to be willing to resign himself to the status quo, as it were, the narrator also sums up his "affair" with Ellen:

As for the madness with Madame Olenska, Archer trained himself to remember it as the last of his discarded experiments. She remained in his memory as the most plaintive and poignant of a line of ghosts.

A year and a half goes by in apparent marital bliss. Is Newland happy? He seems so on the surface, but things may not be what they appear to be. The appearances for whose sake, in fact, the whole society we are dealing with is capable of sacrificing anything and everything may not have any substance behind them. "What if [May's] calm," the narrator remarks, "her niceness, were just a negation, a curtain dropped in front of an emptiness? Archer felt he had never yet lifted that curtain."

When Newland and May visit Mrs. Mignott at one point it appears that Ellen, who has been away all this while, is there for a visit, too. In fact, Mrs. Mignott asks Newland to "fetch her," for she has reportedly walked down to the shore. Newland follows her there and sees her standing at the end of a pier. He does not walk to her because she does not turn around. But that vision of her standing with her back towards him has been enough to rekindle old passions. When Newland hears that Ellen is staying with the Blenkers, relatives of Sillerton Jackson, he goes to the country in search of her under the pretence that he is interested in buying a horse. To his consternation he finds that Ellen has gone to Boston for a few days. He follows her there and they spend the day together. Ellen has come to Boston to meet the secretary who has come with an offer from Europe. Ellen doesn't wish to return there. She tells Newland that she wants to stay in America because of him. They now openly talk of their love for each other, but Ellen is not willing to undo the sacrifice they have undertaken to protect May's happiness. Newland reminds her that it was she who first gave him a "glimpse of a real life" and then asked him "to go on with the false one." Things have not been quite this simple, of course, but Ellen is willing to continue to "endure" the unendurable.

To compound matters, the secretary comes to call on Newland (and he turns out to be the same Frenchman May thought of as "common") and implores him not to let Ellen return to Europe (it would take her to a "false" life, if you will). Newland, in his heart of hearts, has a vested interest in keeping Ellen in America, for it enables them to see each other, even if innocently, from time to time, a thing that helps make the unendurable endurable for him, too, in a certain way, though by now

Newland isn't just amenable to avail himself of chance opportunities, he is now ready to create some. As when he tells May that he is scheduled to go to Washington on business while in reality he merely wants to go there just to see Ellen.

It appears that May suspects this very thing. She certainly cross-examines Newland and seems to catch him in a lie. When Mrs. Mignott has a stroke, Ellen comes to New York from Washington, so Newland's trip there is now pointless. When he tells May that the case has been postponed, she informs him that his boss has gone to Washington to attend to the very case in question. Newland "saves" himself by saying that it wasn't the case itself that was postponed, just his going.

As luck would have it, it is Newland who is to go pick up Ellen at the train station. The trip in the carriage is another chance for them to indulge their irrepressible love for each other. Again, the question of a mere affair arises and is rejected. Ellen doesn't think she should live with Newland as his mistress. When Newland says that he would like to go with her somewhere where such words don't exist, Ellen asks, "Where is that country? Have you ever been there? Is there anywhere we can be happy behind the backs of people who trust us?" Here Newland admits that he is "beyond caring about that." "No you're not!" says Ellen, "You've never been beyond that. I have. I know what it looks like. [A lie in every silence.] It's no place for us." The phrase in brackets, "a lie in every silence," is in the screenplay but is not used in the movie. Yet it more tellingly than anything else sums up the dynamic of any and all illicit love relations, adulterous alliances.

Newland is now ready to act. He seems unable to resist the temptation of acting on his love for Ellen. And by now Ellen relents as well, though not without a certain ambiguity. When she finally asks whether she "should come to" Newland "once, and then go home," Newland indicates that he would prefer this. At this point there is a line in the screenplay that may or may not be acted in such a way as to be clearly perceptible by the viewers. It says: "They look at each other almost like enemies." It's as if finally to be willing to act on their love were both something irresistible and yet unwelcome, a breach not of the usual conduct but of their own private resolve to sacrifice themselves not on the altar of conventions, but on that of their own personal integrity.

The question that the story never answers is whether or not this sacrifice is worth making. Who is its beneficiary? The very conventions that block the fulfillment of what is obviously a case of true love? Or May herself? Would she not have survived a life without Newland? Her innocence (the "innocence that seals the mind against imagination and the heart against experience") is never, of course, annihilated, but she is not above "playing games" in deadly earnest, she is not above trapping Newland in a conventional marriage as against the possibility of a fulfilled love, passionate and irresistible.

When Newland tries to tell May that he wants "out," that he wants to travel and go far away for a while, and when he broaches the subject of Ellen, May's response is to ask why they need to talk of her "now that it's all over." It is from May that Newland learns that Ellen has suddenly changed her mind and is going to return to Europe. To rub salt into the wound, it is May who arranges a farewell dinner for "Countess Olenska" at their own house. It is at the dinner that Newland realizes that he is the victim of a "band of quiet conspirators." It is here that he comes to understand that somehow "the separation between himself and the partner of his guilt had been achieved. And he knew that now the whole tribe had rallied around his wife. He was a prisoner in the center of an armed camp." As the narrator further points out, "from the seamless performance of this ritual, Archer knew that New York believed him to be Madame Olenska's lover. And he understood, for the first time, that his wife shared the belief."

The irony of ironies is that although Newland and Ellen had committed adultery in their hearts, they have not in fact done so, not in reality. And Newland isn't ready to throw in the towel either just yet. Once more, alone with May, he tries to talk to her about his need to travel, to go far away. It is here that May plays her trump card, her pregnancy. The movie is not implying that there is anything insidious about her pregnancy per say, but the way she uses and manipulates it clearly indicates that in spite of the fact that her innocence (the "innocence that seals the mind against imagination and the heart against experience") is never shattered, she is not above "cheating" in her own way and in her own behalf.

May lets Newland guess that the reason why she cannot possibly travel with him is because she is pregnant (she ignores the fact that he wasn't going to want to travel with her). Her manipulation becomes clear to him when she tells him that she has informed Ellen about this as well as her mother and mother-in-law. That was two weeks prior to this, whereas she has just then told Newland that she wasn't sure about her pregnancy until the morning of that very day. This final "trap" works. Newland is now tied to her for life. And, as the screenplay tells us, May's "eyes are wet with VICTORY" (capitals in original).

The final part of the movie now commences. It is an afterthought as well as a denouement. The narrator informs us that Newland remained a "dutiful, loving father, and a faithful husband." We also learn that May, now dead, a victim of "infectious pneumonia," was never disabused of any of her illusions, so much so that her children, the same as Newland, had always concealed their true views from her. We also learn that Newland had honestly mourned her when she passed on. When his grown son drags him to Paris with him, Newland is 57 years old. It is from his son that he finds out that the day before May died she told him (the son) how once when she "asked" him, Newland "gave up the thing" he "wanted most." This information moves Newland deeply, for indeed throughout his life with May "whenever he thought of Ellen Olenska," she was always "the complete vision of all that he had missed."

There is something heart-rending about the ending of the story, which (again) operates on a number of different levels. Why does Newland refuse to go up to Ellen's Paris apartment? He sits in front of her building on a bench while his son proceeds to go upstairs to meet the "woman" his father once "almost threw everything over for." He remains seated on the bench, looking up at Ellen Olenska's window until the light of the setting sun flares up and the vision changes to the time she stood on the pier in the distance with her back turned towards him. This time, however, she turns around and looks straight into the camera. Newland then gets up and slowly walks away, with the aid of a cane.

Again, the question arises: has he done the right thing? Where does a person's true duty lie? With the "values of the tribe"? Or with the demands of his or her own heart? The human condition is replete with the age-old conflict between the individual and society. Neither the novel nor the movie can give us an adequate answer. All I know is that every time I watch this movie (and the last time I saw it was not—I am sure—the last time), I always finish it with an uneasy feeling and a poignant regret, a regret so deep that it's hard to fathom its ultimate import. I am sure I am not the only one who feels that, in spite of everything, Newland shouldn't have missed out on Ellen. At the same time, the question persists: could he (can any of us) buy happiness at the expense of others? Didn't May?

2. City of Angels

[Movie Log: Released in 1989 by Warner Brothers. Screenplay by Dana Stevens, based on *Wings of Desire* by Wim Wenders. Directed by Brad Silberling. Cast: Nicholas Cage (Seth); Meg Ryan (Maggie); André Braugher (Cassiel); Dennis Franz (Mr. Messinger); Colm Feore (Jordan); Robin Bartlett (Anne)]

> *The greatest poverty is not to live*
> *In a physical world, to feel that one's desire*
> *Is too difficult to tell from despair*
> —Wallace Stevens

City of Angels is not simply a remake of *Wings of Desire* (*Der Himmel über Berlin*, 1987). What the two movies have in common is the basic plot of an angel falling in love with a woman and then falling into humanity for her sake. The stories are otherwise different. And their ending is completely different. There are certain commonalities between them and I shall point some of these out later. *City of Angels* utilizes two traditional ideas each of which has its roots in classical antiquity. One of these is the so-called Great Chain of Being and the other is the Music of the Spheres. And, of course, the title is a charming pun on the name of Los Angeles where the story takes place and where Hollywood is also located.

The Great Chain of Being has a long history. What's relevant of it for an appreciative understanding of *City of Angels* can be summarized briefly. There is a hierarchy in the world according to which angels are above humans who are above animals who are above plant life. The trick is that the level above each level lacks something that the one below it has. Which is why angels may envy the human experience of physical reality. The experience in question goes beyond the five senses, it includes human love, for example, particularly the romantic kind. (The English title of *Wings of Desire* is clearly an allusion to this angelic envy of the human.)

The other idea that plays a prominent role in *City of Angels* is the Music of the Spheres. This is what the angels hear when they gather by the ocean at sunrise and sunset. Human beings cannot hear this heavenly music (though according to certain old tenets the pure of heart could), but they can feel things that angels cannot feel. Angels cannot touch or taste. They cannot feel the wind in their faces or water against their bodies.

The primary role of angels in *City of Angels* is to collect the souls of the dying. They hover above humans, sometimes get very close to them and read their thoughts (as they also do in *Wings of Desire*), but they don't necessarily function as guardian angels in the traditional sense. They come close to this at times, as when Seth and Cassiel seem to keep things from getting ugly during a hold-up in a store.

We first see Seth when he comes for the soul of a dying girl. This first scene (a prologue in that it comes before the credits) sets the stage for one of the functions of *City of Angels*, a function the movie has in common with almost all forms of religiosity: an assurance that death is but the passing into another kind of life, a passing from a physical to a spiritual existence. There is a paradox in this that the movie does not resolve. I will come back to it in the end. In any event, this first episode utilizes a popular image that so-called near-death experiences have in common, the light at the end of the tunnel. As Seth and the spirit of the young girl walk hand in hand through a corridor of the hospital, a bright light appears at the end of this tunnel-like structure that becomes ever brighter and ever more intense as Seth and the spirit of the girl finally disappear in it.

Seth asks the little girl what she liked best, presumably in the life she has just left behind. And she says "pajamas." Seth reports this to Cassiel, the fellow angel he frequently hangs out with. They think it's an interesting answer, one that reflects on the unique nature of individual human beings and on the apparently inexplicable penchant that humans have for particular preferences. Seth also wonders what human touch would be like, a sign that he has more than the typical angelic interest in humanity. He wonders, in fact, about what it would be like to be human. For, as Cassiel makes it clear (after Seth has mentioned the little girl's desire for wings), "Angels aren't human. We were never human." (The implication is that human beings don't become angels after death either.)

All this is happening rather fast in movie-time (my writing-time goes more slowly for now). We next see Maggie (M. Rice, M.D.) arrive at the hospital on a bicycle. She is young, energetic, and confident. She is about to perform open-heart surgery on a 50-year-old man. The operation is routine. But no sooner is it completed than the patient's heart develops a fatal arrhythmia. It is during Maggie's frantic attempts to bring the man back to life that Seth (who is there to collect the man's spirit) falls in love with Maggie.

49

We see Maggie as she is massaging the exposed heart of the man in an attempt to restore his heartbeat. Someone says that "he is going." Maggie exclaims that "He is not going anywhere!" At that precise moment she seems to look straight into Seth's eyes. It seems to Seth that she sees him (though he probably knows better) and it is at this precise moment that he seems to fall in love with her (though he probably doesn't realize this just yet). This scene is also important for reasons that are not immediately obvious. With Maggie and Seth seemingly looking at each other, we see an interaction between the physical and the spiritual where the unbelieving Maggie and the angelic Seth suddenly take on more significance than each has individually. The whole they represent at this moment is somehow greater than the sum of its parts, as if the severance between the physical and the spiritual were merely an illusion.

This moment is pivotal in Maggie's life. As a doctor, she is practically an atheist. She believes in this life and in this life only, and she fights to the best of her ability to keep it going. But in spite of the "textbook" nature of the operation, the patient dies. Inexplicably. Later Maggie will speak of her sudden feeling this experience has given her, that "none of this is in [her] hands." Later still she will tell Seth that she feels there is "something bigger out there," a sign that she is ready to recognize the supernatural. But her empirical, practical, materialistic view of life will not be given up without a fight.

Next we see Maggie helpless in front of the departed man's wife and daughter. The loss of this patient shakes her to the core of her being. She runs into a stairwell and she cries and talks to herself, unable to comprehend why what has happened has happened. The sudden loss of control over life and death does not agree with her medical expertise. Seth is there, facing her, trying to comfort her, though invisible and imperceptible by her. Later we see Maggie stand alone in the operating room staring at the empty operating table. Later still we see her throw up.

The next operation she is to perform (an operation on a certain Mr. Messinger) is postponed. She doesn't appear up to it to certain of her colleagues. Seth is still hanging around Maggie as she talks to Jordan, a fellow doctor and her boyfriend. Seth seems shocked to discover this relationship, almost as if he were jealous of Jordan. Then we see Seth in the library. He hovers over people. At one point he sits across from an old man overhearing the words the old man is reading from Hemingway's *A Movable Feast*. The words bear an odd relevance to *City of Angels*:

You expected to be sad in the fall. Part of you died each year when the leaves fell from the trees and their branches were bare against the wind and the cold, wintry light. But you knew there would always be the spring, as you knew the river would flow again after it was frozen. When the cold rains kept on and killed the spring, it was as though a young person had died for no reason.

Later Seth will place this book on Maggie's nightstand who will assume that it came from Jordan or perhaps a patient. In the interim Seth learns from Cassiel that he can make himself appear to human beings if he wishes. What it interesting about this (and about other instances involving Seth learning new things) is that it goes against the grain of traditional angel lore. One of the things about angels in comparison to people is that they can't learn anything because they already know everything. People, on the other hand, do learn new things all the time. Without the ability to learn people would remain woefully ignorant (many choose to be, but that's another story). But there is more to learning than mere necessity. Learning entails a sense of wonder, even a sense of child-like wonder that some people never outgrow. This is part of what angels envy human beings for.

Speaking of learning, just moments before Seth appears to Maggie "in person," we see her in her study pouring over medical books. When she comes out into the hallway, she sees Seth for the first time. She thinks he is a visitor (which, of course, he is but not the kind she imagines him to be) and informs him that visiting hours are over. She assumes that he has been visiting with Mr. Messinger, but he asks her whether *she* is in despair. Maggie indicates that she lost a patient. When Seth says that "he is living, just not the way you think," Maggie responds with: "I don't believe in that." Seth tells her that "some things are true whether you believe in them or not."

Maggie is obviously attracted to Seth, though at this point not necessarily as a woman would be attracted to a man. There is nevertheless something oddly appealing about Seth to her. When she wants to know how he knows her name, Seth points to her nametag. Later, at her locker, she will look at it herself and see that it doesn't say "Maggie," just "M. Rice, M.D." Maggie doesn't make much of this mystery (though it obviously strikes her as odd), even as she didn't make much of the mystery of Seth's sudden disappearance. When she walks away from him after their initial encounter, she turns back to take another look at him, but he is no longer there. She turns back several more times, clearly puzzled.

Mr. Messinger's operation goes well. This restores Maggie's confidence. We see her take a leisurely bath (Seth is there, though invisible again) then we see her wake up at 3:14 in the morning. She finds *A Movable Feast* on her nightstand. The oddity of this strikes her, though she reads part of the book, perhaps the passage about spring (which she later mentions to Jordan), which ends with the words "as though a young person had died for no reason."

In the library, where she goes to find out who the book has been issued to, she runs into Seth again. This encounter is once more both an encounter between the material and the spiritual on a philosophic plane and also very much like the typical beginning of the typical romance. In any event, when asked what he does for a living, Seth tells Maggie that he is a messenger. To further promptings for additional information Seth actually tells her the truth ("I am a messenger of God"—note that the etymological meaning of the word "angel" is messenger) but Maggie obviously doesn't take this literally, it strikes her as merely a charming witticism.

It is at this point that the encounter becomes reminiscent of the commencement of a typical this-worldly romance. Seth: "Let's go somewhere." Maggie: "Where?" Seth: "I don't care." Maggie: "What do you want to do?" Seth: "Anything." This is very romantic (even when we recognize the dialogue as an echo from *Valley Girl*, 1983). In any case, it is obvious that what's important to Seth is to simply be in Maggie's company. His angelic curiosity about the human experience of physical reality continues in the charming scene with the pear. Earlier, while still in the library, Seth reads a passage from Hemingway about the taste of oysters. Now he wants to know what a pear tastes like to Maggie. Her response that it is "sweet, juicy, soft on your tongue, grainy, like sugary sand that melts in your mouth" pleases Seth a lot.

The next scene finds the two in a lab where Maggie shows Seth a drop of her blood under a microscope. Once again we witness an encounter between the material and the spiritual. Maggie seems to think that there is nothing beyond the cells that constitute our bodies. Though it is here that she also makes the statement about her newly acquired feeling that "there is something bigger out there." This leads to several interesting scenes. Maggie's beeper sounds, indicating an emergency. She rushes up to Mr.

Messinger's room. Seth goes there, too, once more invisible like the angel he is. It appears that Mr. Messinger was choking on a blocked breathing tube. A false alarm. What's interesting about this scene is that Seth seems puzzled at first. It appears that Mr. Messinger's life is on the line for a moment even though Seth knows that this is not the case.

This immediately leads to a second scene, which carries a great deal of weight in the story (and it is also an echo of a thematically similar scene from *Wings of Desire*). As Seth, in his invisible, angelic form, is about to leave the room, Mr. Messinger suddenly says, "I can't see you, but I know you are there." It is in the aftermath of this scene that Seth learns from Mr. Messinger about the possibility of taking the plunge, of falling into humanity. And it should be pointed out that Messinger's name is a dead give-away. For, as I mentioned before, the etymological meaning of "angel" is, of course, messenger. (The variation in the spelling of Messinger's name—which may not be obvious to moviegoers—is perhaps a visual indicator that he is no longer an angel.) The scene in the cafeteria where Mr. Messinger can't seem to get enough food, for example, is replete with the former angel's inordinate enjoyment of earthly existence. This scene is of even more importance, though, for it leads to a number of other discussions between Seth and Mr. Messinger during which Seth learns that, having been endowed with free will just like human beings, he can, as an angel, choose to "fall" into humanity and become mortal.

Maggie is given a number of signs that what she is dealing with is not what appears to be. At Messinger's get-well party, for example, someone takes a Polaroid shot of Seth and Messinger's daughter. Seth's image does not appear on the picture though. He appears simply washed out, like a streak of light. Maggie, once more, looks puzzled but does not make much of the fact. It is not until they are in Maggie's kitchen and Seth is cutting up a head of lettuce that Maggie notices something so extraordinary that her reaction to it is downright shocking. Seth cuts through his thumb without in any way injuring it. Maggie picks up a knife and cuts into Seth's hand (without in any way injuring it). It is here that Seth tells her who he really is. That he "met" her when he came to take Mr. Balford (the patient Maggie lost just after operating on him) and that he has been appearing to Maggie in human form because he is in love with her. Maggie's immediate reaction is that she "cannot conceive of" this. Meaning, the existence of a hereafter, of a heaven and of angels.

Things now move rapidly. Seth discusses the possibility of falling into humanity with Cassiel. Maggie operates again. At night she sleeps restlessly while the song "In the Arms of an Angel" plays in the background. This is followed by a rainy night when Seth, once more invisible, comes to spend the night with Maggie. The morning after Maggie seems to have a sudden insight into what's wrong with an abandoned infant her friend and colleague, Ann, has been attending to in the hospital's pediatric ward. She doesn't know why she suddenly realized what was wrong with the baby, she just knows. The fact that the baby can't breath properly is yet another subtle reminder that the physical is tied to the spiritual since etymologically "spirit" means "breath."

The next scene is in the locker room with Jordan who wants to marry Maggie, partly on the grounds that they are "the same species." Messinger later tells Maggie that Seth could fall into humanity if he wanted to. Maggie goes to the library to find Seth. She calls out to him and he appears to her. Seth tells Maggie that she doesn't love Jordan. Her response is that he and she "are the same." She also tells Seth that she doesn't want to see him again. Which sounds like a kind of ultimatum, but it has a more subtle function in what follows. For what follows is that Seth takes the "plunge," the "fall." That he does so uncertain of his future with Maggie makes his plunge or fall somehow more heroic. The fall, an actual physical fall, does leave its mark on Seth in terms of cuts and bruises (though an ordinary mortal would probably have perished in the attempt). And once fallen, he can no longer just "fly through the air" and appear wherever he wants to. He has to walk, which he does with exuberance and joy to the tune of "that old black magic of love."

In the hospital, where he comes in search of Maggie, he tells Ann, who is attending to his wounds, that he "fell in love." Ann tells him that he may find Maggie at Lake Tahoe on the Nevada side. With that information Seth sets out on his journey. He hitches a ride with a truck driver in the rain and barefoot (some thugs have ripped off his boots in a scene just before). The song in the background during the drive seems to capture Seth's feelings at the moment: "I'd give up forever to touch you" or "you're the closest to heaven that I'll ever be" and "I just don't want to miss you tonight."

Arriving at Maggie's hide-out at Lake Tahoe begins the fulfillment of Seth's earthly desires. Maggie tells Seth that she couldn't marry Jordan because she is in love with Seth while Seth tells Maggie that his being there is a result of "free will." As they lie by a cozy fire and as Maggie attends to Seth's cuts and bruises, their long night of lovemaking begins. The morning finds them at lakeside where they talk of their plans for the future, thinking that they have their whole lives ahead of them.

As Seth is taking a shower, savoring every moment of it (even though at first he almost scalds himself), Maggie rushes off to a nearby store for last-minute breakfast preparations. On the way home on her bicycle a truck suddenly pulls out in front of her and she collides with it. At that precise moment Seth notices a candle blow out on the breakfast table. He senses that something is wrong and runs out to find Maggie lying on the road on her back on make-shift bedding. The driver of the truck has gone for help.

This is a heart-breaking scene (and I have talked with people who don't like the ending of this movie at all). Seth is no longer an angel, but he knows that an angel is probably there to collect Maggie's spirit. He tells her not to look at "them." Maggie says that she is not afraid any more and that "when they ask me what I liked best, I'll tell them it was you." This is an echo of the first scene where Seth asks the little girl who has just died what she had liked best. I find this connection between the beginning and the ending poignant.

In the aftermath of Maggie's death Cassiel comes to show himself to Seth. The latter is angry and even considers the possibility that he has been punished, though Cassiel tells him that he ought to know better. Cassiel wants to know whether Seth would have fallen into humanity if he had known that Maggie was going to die so soon. He says that "I would rather have had one breath of her hair, one kiss of her mouth, one touch of her hand, than eternity without it."

In the final scenes we see Seth bite into the same kind of pear the taste of which Maggie had first described to him earlier. Then we see him rush into the ocean to encounter the feel of earthly existence as his formerly fellow angels (including Cassiel) stand by the shore listening to the Music of the Spheres. Cassiel's smile indicates a vicarious enjoyment of Seth's physical experience as the latter swims in the ocean.

So what does this ending signify? Why couldn't Seth and Maggie live happily ever after, in proper fairy-tale fashion? The story of *Wings of Desire* ends like that, with the promise of a long life of marital and earthly bliss. Why have Seth and Maggie been denied this? Why is it all taken away from them after just one night of happiness?

Here we have to assume that in a work of art things don't just happen without rhyme or reason. There must, therefore, be something thematically significant in this ending even though it may frustrate many viewers. There have been two things that have appealed to Seth (the angel) about an earthly existence all along: human love and "the touch of earthly years" (to borrow a phrase from Wordsworth). He has lost the first but he can retain the latter, though only for a while. Cassiel tries to explain Maggie's death to him by saying that Seth is alive now and that someday he will die, too. This ending touches upon a deeper mystery, one that we simply must live with. It doesn't seem that the eternal life of angels is life as we know it, which is why some of them, according to the angel lore repeated by the movie, will give up eternity for this life which is precious and beautiful perhaps precisely because, like all earthly love, it cannot last forever. The paradox doesn't stop with the fact that after this life comes another, one that promises to be immortal. Will that be an eternity from which we will long to return to this life, which we may forever desire precisely because it is always already passing strange?

3. As Good As It Gets

[Movie Log: Released in 1998 by TriStar Pictures. Screenplay by Mark Andrus and James L. Brooks. Directed by James L. Brooks. Cast: Jack Nicholson (Melvin Udall); Helen Hunt (Carol Conneley); Greg Kinnear (Simon Bishop); Cuba Gooding, Jr. (Frank Sachs); Shirley Knight (Beverly); Jesse James (1) (Spencer Conneley); Harold Ramis (Dr. Martin Bettes)]

> *In hell, and earth, and seas, and heavens above,*
> *Love conquers all; and we must yield to love.*
> —Vergil, Eclogue 10, Gallus

The first thing we see is a sweet older woman's reaction to Melvin Udall. More precisely, we see the woman in question standing in the open doorway of her apartment, talking to someone in the apartment (presumably her husband), telling this unseen person that she is going out to buy some flowers and that she is very happy. Then she suddenly changes her mind, retreats into the apartment and closes the door in disgust.

It is at this point that we find the cause of her sudden change of mind. We now see Melvin Udall trying to entice his neighbor's dog, Verdell, in the hallway. Once he succeeds, we see what his intentions have been all along. He unceremoniously throws the frightened little dog down the garbage chute, presumably for urinating in the hallway. When Simon Bishop, Verdell's owner, comes looking for his little dog, Melvin pretends not to know what he is talking about. When he can no longer pretend to be mistaken he says, ironically, "Hope you find him. I love that dog." "You don't love anything, Mr. Udall," says Simon.

The rest of the movie is, in fact, the slow unfolding of how love comes to Melvin, this "creepy" and obnoxious character who, besides suffering from a high dose of misanthropy (with a good measure of misogyny thrown in), is also the victim of a case of impulsive-compulsive behavior. Love comes to him unbeknownst to him and in such a way that he is the last person to know it. The irony is that he is a successful writer of romances—that is, love stories. In fact, when Simon comes knocking on his door (for he suspects that Melvin is responsible for Verdell's ending up in the basement), he is trying to find the right word for a sentence beginning with the words "Love was—"

Melvin's response to this interruption of his creative endeavors is a splendid example of his utter unfriendliness, though it is far from the kind of foot-in-the-mouth blunder that almost gets him barred from his favorite restaurant, the only place where he seems to be "at home," where there is a waitress, Carol Conneley, the only person who knows how to deal with him, and the only person Melvin seems to tolerate. The first time he really puts his foot in his mouth is when he tells her that her son is sure to die. This is an extremely callous and uncalled-for remark, and Carol lets him know it, too, in no uncertain terms. The interesting thing about this scene (and others where Melvin also puts his foot into his mouth) is that no sooner are the unkind words out of his mouth than he knows that he has misspoken, that he has said something awful that he simply should never ever have said. But, of course, it is too late. The words cannot be unsaid.

The slow unfolding of how love comes to Melvin Udall begins its insinuative thread when Simon Bishop's male model lets his criminal friends rob Simon's place. When Simon, thanks to Verdell's barking and carrying on, catches the burglars in the act, they beat him to within an inch of his life. It is when Verdell needs someone to take care of him and when Simon's black friend (and—presumably—lover, too), Frank Sachs, decides that the person who should have the honor must absolutely be Melvin, that love enters Melvin's life through the metaphorical back door.

Melvin's first reaction to the presence of the little dog in his apartment is one of horror. Soon, however, he places food in Verdell's dish and, when the mistrustful little dog is slow to approach it, he begins to play the piano for the dog as a kind of equivalent of whistling in the dark in order to allay someone's fear of it: "Always look on the bright side of life." Soon, without becoming fully conscious of the fact just yet, Melvin begins to love the little dog. This becomes obvious when Melvin notices that, like he himself, Verdell (a fast learner) is also avoiding stepping on cracks in the sidewalk. "Don't you be like me!" he exclaims, as he picks the little dog up and lifts him high with tender loving care. Even passers-by notice his kindly disposition towards Verdell.

As the story progresses and we gain insight into Melvin, we also get glimpses into Carol's life. Her date with a young man who, upon returning to her apartment with her, is ready to make love to her goes awry when Spencer, her asthmatic son, coughs and the proceedings are thus temporarily interrupted. The young man finds the "little bit of throw-up" on Carol's dress in the aftermath of the interruption "too much reality" for a romantic (or at least lust-filled) date and leaves. In the meantime we also get a glimpse into the life of Simon as well. The theory of his art is revealed when he tells his model (who will be indirectly responsible for the subsequent robbery that will get his life tangled up with that of Melvin's through Verdell, the dog) that he watches people because when one watches someone long enough, their humanity is revealed. Which is why he doesn't require his models to strike any specific pose. Once they are caught, as it were, in a certain characteristic stance, Simon paints them.

The set-up to the story, therefore, involves three (four with Verdell) main characters: Melvin Udall, the misanthropic and impulsive-compulsive writer of romances, Carol Conneley, the single-mother waitress with the asthmatic son, and Simon Bishop, the homosexual artist and his little dog, Verdell. It's clear from the beginning that Carol has a special "power" over Melvin. He is used to her waiting on him and, due to his impulsive-compulsive condition, he *must* sit at the same table and *must* have Carol wait on him each time he goes to the restaurant where she works.

Once Verdell ends up with Melvin, things begin to change, as love slowly but surely makes headway in his life. By the time the severely beaten Simon returns from the hospital and finds himself in financial ruins, Verdell has done his part. When the time comes for Melvin to return the dog, he knows that he has been "stricken." This is apparent as we watch him play the piano and as his laughter turns to crying "over a dog, over an ugly dog."

This crisis is followed by Melvin's unscheduled visit to his doctor's office. It is here, after his doctor refuses to accommodate him on the spur of the moment, that the movie's title is utilized when Melvin, in an apparent moment of malice, tells the patients in the doctor's waiting room, "What if this is as good as it gets?" But this crisis is merely the first in a series. When Melvin gets to his regular restaurant, he finds that Carol is not there. He is so rude to the substitute waitress that the owner throws him out (to the applause of the other patrons—for it is clear that Melvin is disliked by many), though not before he manages to "bribe" an employee for Carol's home address.

Carol is, of course, shocked to see Melvin show up at her door. In her no-nonsense treatment of Melvin she tells him, in no uncertain terms, how "creepy" his behavior is. And at this point Melvin's bad luck hasn't run its course yet. When he instructs Spencer to "answer" when talked to, Carol, too, throws him out. But the third time (first the doctor, then the restaurant's owner and now Carol) is a charm of sorts. When Spencer needs to be rushed to the hospital, Carol catches up with the departing Melvin and commandeers his cab.

It is in the hospital that the idea of getting his publisher's husband (who happens to be a doctor) to take care of Spencer comes to Melvin. His sole motive appears to be selfish, to get Carol back to work, so things can get back to "normal" in his life. In the meantime, Simon finds out that he is broke as well as that Verdell misses Melvin. Though in arranging for Spencer's medical care Melvin is performing an act of kindness, his obnoxious nature is still in full swing. When, for example, a secretary at the publishing house wants to know how he manages to write about women so well, Melvin's response is that when he creates a female character he just thinks of a man without "reason and accountability."

When, upon returning home, Carol notices a car with an M.D. license plate parked in front of her house, she panics. Upon learning of the source of the "gift" (namely, that Melvin Udall wants to be billed for Spencer's medical expenses), she goes ballistic (though not before giving, according to Dr. Bettes, her insurance company's famous—or should it be infamous— "technical name": "fucking HMO bastard pieces of shit"). The word "crazy" is now used twice in two scenes back to back. First Melvin tells Simon's departing maid to "sell crazy some place else" (in response to her talk of the joys of life Simon needs reminders of), and then we are back in Carol's apartment where she shouts at her mother that the arrangement made by Melvin lets a "crazy man" into their lives.

Melvin's acts of kindness now come in fairly rapid succession. Though not without acts of selfishness thrown into the bargain. When he returns to Simon's apartment upon walking Verdell, he tries to cheer up this "absolute horror of a human being" (as Simon refers to himself in a moment of utter despair) by explaining that Verdell's preference for him is a "trick" due to Melvin's constantly feeding him bits of bacon. The proof fails, though, for even when Simon holds the bacon, Verdell still goes to Melvin. The close-up of their faces (the man's and the dog's) reveals a remarkable similarity between Melvin and Verdell; they look alike the way some pets and their owners are said to eventually come to resemble each other.

Carol, who suspects that Melvin has designs on her body, now rushes to Melvin's apartment late in the evening. When she arrives, she looks as if she had entered a wet T-shirt contest (due to the rainfall that catches her off guard on her way to Melvin's). The encounter between Carol and Melvin is telling. She thinks his having arranged for Spencer's medical treatment for the sole purpose of getting her to come back to work so she can wait on him is utterly strange, so she tells him, in no uncertain terms, that she is never going to "sleep with [him]."

At this point Melvin begins to show the unmistakable symptoms of being in love. He can't sleep. He takes Chinese soup to Simon. He is in love and he doesn't know it. Meanwhile Carol is working on a thank-you note, which (the next day) Melvin refuses to accept. It is here that Frank offers his convertible so that Melvin might take Simon to Baltimore, where Simon's parents live, in order to see if they (Simon's parents) will help out Simon financially. At first Melvin resists the offer of this trip, but then he thinks that if Carol were to come along with them, he would be interested.

When Frank leaves, Carol returns with the thank-you note from which she at first reads parts and then the whole thing. Melvin is obviously uncomfortable in the presence of this emotion-filled expression of gratitude. But when Carol finishes he nonetheless makes a pitch for her to accompany them on the trip to Baltimore. She hesitates at first, but he "blackmails" her into agreeing to the trip.

The trip continues the good-moves/bad moves unfolding of the friendship and love between Carol and Melvin. Carol and Simon obviously hit it off, both being friendly and kindly predisposed souls. They gang up on Melvin a bit, too, here and there. When they settle into their lodgings in Baltimore, and when Carol learns over the phone that Spencer is doing well, and so finds herself in a very good mood, she decides that Melvin will be her date for the night (Simon is too tired and tense to go out).

In the restaurant (where Melvin is overly anxious to have a nice crab dinner), he once more puts his foot in his mouth. Carol obviously finds him very attractive and even kisses him on the mouth. Melvin seems happy. But he says the wrong thing when he refers to the fact that he had to go buy a coat and tie in order to be admitted to the restaurant while they let Carol in in a "housecoat." When Carol demands a compliment else she will leave, Melvin rises to the occasion, though the compliment's true significance is couched in such terms as to even escape Carol herself at first, but when she hears that Melvin has begun to take pills (a thing he absolutely hates doing) because he wants to be a better man for Carol's sake, she is deeply touched.

But he ruins the whole evening when in response to her question as to why he wanted her along for this trip, Melvin says that he thought that if she and Simon had sex then perhaps Simon wouldn't hit on him. He doesn't, of course, get a chance to finish this sentence, which is an utterly bizarre and ridiculous and incredibly insensitive and even stupid thing to have said. The words uttered, though, cannot be unsaid. This time Carol leaves. Back at their lodgings she moves into Simon's room. Simon decides to draw her while watching her from bed as she sits on the edge of the bathtub. At first she is reluctant to be Simon's model, but then she succumbs to the charm of the situation. Also, this act is restorative of Simon's willingness to start working again. Carol and Simon truly enjoy this sudden outburst of creativity on Simon's part.

The next morning Melvin rushes into their room demanding to know whether they had sex or not. They have not, of course, though (as Carol says) what they had was better than sex. The trip home is joyless. And once they get there (where Simon is in the dark as to who will put him off temporarily, as he has now been evicted from his apartment), Carol refuses to let Melvin take her home. In fact, she tells him that in spite of his kindness to Spencer, she no longer wants to know him. To Simon's surprise, it is Melvin who will temporarily lodge him in his own apartment. Carol feels guilty about having broken off the relationship with Melvin, so she calls his number. Simon answers the phone, so she learns of this additional act of kindness on Melvin's part. She tells him how terrible she feels about having ended their relationship, but she still doesn't want to see him any more, in spite of the "extraordinary kindnesses that took place."

It is now Simon who gives Melvin the final encouragement to act. He must act and not sleep over the matter. He knows that he loves Carol. He must go to her tonight, now, immediately. Melvin does precisely that. When Carol wants to know why he has come, he says, "I had to see you." Carol's mother is overjoyed at hearing this (she is eavesdropping behind the open door to Carol's apartment). When Carol expresses a desire for a "normal boyfriend" (and her mother tells her that everybody wants that but there is no such thing), the fact that Carol has spoken of him as a "boyfriend" does not escape Melvin.

The story now reaches its climax and the promise of a happily ever-aftering conclusion. Though even here the back-and-forth between bad and good moves proliferates (hopefully for the last time). Though it's four in the morning, Melvin wants to go take a walk with Carol. Once outside (on the pretext that there is a bakery nearby, which is presumably to open soon and which, therefore, means that they are not nuts for taking a walk so early in the morning, just people who like "warm rolls"), Melvin is still avoiding the cracks in the sidewalk. Carol is once more ready to call the whole thing off.

It is here that Melvin pays her the ultimate compliment. He tells her that he thinks of her as the greatest woman in the world. And he says he wonders why other people don't notice this about her. And he also says that he is proud of the fact that he knows it, for it makes him feel good about himself. Carol finally recognizes that Melvin really loves her. They kiss and proceed towards the bakery that's just opening (for warm rolls). As they enter, Melvin is forced to step on a crack in the sidewalk right in front of the bakery. It's obvious to the viewer that this doesn't escape his notice, and the screenplay verifies the viewer's suspicion that he is "cured" by stating that Melvin "registers the momentous fact."

Thus it is now that everything is as good as it gets. Love has, indeed, conquered all in this movie. And the movement has been towards charitable acts all along, so that things really began with what we might see as agape rather than as eros. Though, of course, once agape (or charity) has done its work, eros has been able to emerge as well. Melvin is indeed a better, a much better man, in the end, thanks to Carol's inadvertent agency, an agency full of the most natural good will and good cheer and (as Melvin himself says in his ultimate compliment to her) in her always saying what she means and always meaning something "that's all about being straight and good." Die-hard realists may not see Melvin as cured in the end, but movies (even realistic ones) have more in common with fairy tales than with psychological case studies, so I go with the poetic faith (which I am willing to extend to real life as well) that love can indeed at times conquer all, even to the tune of performing miracles.

4. American Beauty

[Movie Log: Released in 1999 by Dreamworks Pictures. Screenplay by Alan Ball. Directed by Sam Mendes. Cast: Kevin Spacey (Lester Burnham); Annette Bening (Carol Burnham); Thora Birch (Jane Burnham); Wes Bentley (Ricky Fitts); Mena Suvari (Angela Hayes); Peter Gallagher (Buddy Kane); Chris Cooper (Colonel Fitts); Allison Janney (Barbara Fitts)]

> *O Rose thou art sick!*
> *The invisible worm*
> *That flies in the night*
> *In the howling storm,*
>
> *Has found out thy bed*
> *Of crimson joy,*
> *And his dark secret love*
> *Does thy life destroy.*
> —William Blake

"Ambiguity" isn't the right word to begin this discussion with. Multiple meanings, or meanings on many levels, would be more appropriate. To begin with, the title (though this is not immediately apparent) is the name of a breed of rose. And "rose" is a traditional symbol of love (and can, as Rose, also be the first name of a woman). In certain scenes (usually those involving Lester's sexual fantasies of Angela) rose petals abound. The fact that Lester's de facto estranged wife, Carolyn, breeds roses (obviously of the American Beauty kind), is itself full of ironies.

In addition to being the name of a breed of rose, the title's words may also be taken to refer to Angela, the "American beauty" who captures Lester's lustful heart, even as she recaptures something vital in him that was lost in the American dream which has subtly turned into an American nightmare—the promise of the good life into the soul-killing routine of expensive and widespread materialism. There is an additional use the movie makes of "beauty" (as we shall see) when it functions as part of Ricky's (and eventually of Lester's) *ars poetica*, or (for lack of a better word) theory of art (as well as, in this case, of life, too).

In some sense this movie is about the art of living vs. (for lack of a better term) the "business" of life. It begins with what will turn out to be a disturbing and ominous flash forward, where Jane, Lester's daughter, speaks of her father's lust for Angela as a pathetic something for which someone "really should put him out of his misery." She says this to Ricky, her boyfriend, who happens to be filming her at the moment (Ricky's filming is itself a kind of meta-cinematographic theme that runs through the movie, culminating in Lester's repetition, after his death, of words reminiscent of Ricky's own theory of art and "beauty"—about which more later).

The movie "proper" begins with Lester's voice-over as the camera descends over a tree-lined street (appropriately yet perhaps ironically named Robin Hood Trail). This narratorial voice is atypical in that (as it will turn out), it is actually the voice of the Lester who has already died. The idea that the whole story is told from the point of view of a dead protagonist is reminiscent of *Sunset Boulevard* (1950), which uses a similar ploy. Ambiguity abounds here, too, especially when in addition to "predicting" his own death in less than a year, Lester claims that, "in a way" he is "dead already." Which is both literally and metaphorically true, though at the moment the intended meaning is metaphorical and metaphorical only.

Sex in *American Beauty* symbolizes an essential raw vitality, even when it appears in the form of Lester's masturbation (which is one of the first things we see even as we hear Lester himself openly and honestly admit to it in his morning shower). This vitality stands out in sharp contrast with the deadening of life by suburban living, which artificializes life as opposed to enhancing the art of living (the art of living involves artifice, too, but the commercialized version of suburban life is pure artificiality, a big difference the movie emphasizes over and over again).

Carolyn's cultivation of the rose named American Beauty is, at this point, the sole remnant of something resembling genuine vitality in her, though her gardening equipment (color-coordinated as it is) is a bit much, as Lester observes. As Angela herself will claim later (to Jane), there's something "phony" about Carolyn. She has gone almost completely over to the realm of the artificial and the material. Lester, in his clumsy way, recognizes the loss he himself has suffered along these lines since the beginning of their marriage, as well as since the time he was on good terms with his daughter, and it is fairly early on that, recognizing this loss (something to his credit in the eyes of the movie's audience), he also asserts that it's "never too late to get it back."

From here on, we are in fact witnesses to Lester's attempt to get "it" back. The first sign of this is his willingness to speak his mind. He objects to dishonesty and corruption at his place of work. He speaks out against the sneaky and underhanded ways in which the company he works for, an advertising magazine, goes about trying to justify its "firing" of some of its employees. It is at the dinner table that he brings this last item up. It is interesting to note that though this particular family habitually dines together, to "elevator music"—Carolyn's choice (though the first time what is played in the background is "Bali Ha'i" from *South Pacific* (1958), a song which expresses a desire for a happier life in some "magical elsewhere")—it is obvious, from the way both Carolyn and Jane fail to even feign interest in Lester's critical remarks, that this dining together (ordinarily a sign of genuine family life) has by now been a meaningless ritual in this particular family for who knows how long.

In the aftermath of this scene we see Lester and Jane in the kitchen as Lester makes an honest effort to reconnect with his daughter. And it is here that we suddenly switch to Ricky's filming father and daughter across the drive between their respecting houses, from window to window. Ricky is the son of the Burnhams' new neighbors, the Fittses. Like Lester (and, of course, like the younger generation in general, like both Jane and Angela, in their own ways), Ricky is also genuine and an artist, in fact, a cinematographer of sorts.

The theme of suburban ersatz continues as we see Carolyn prepare for an open house in a somewhat dilapidated neighborhood. A series of potential buyers come, but she fails to make the sale (in spite of desperately trying to pep-talk herself into it). The last couple (probably a pair of lesbians) object to the fact that there is nothing "lagoon-like" in the swimming pool. Though this criticism may be a bit unfair, with a taint of malice to it, it is nevertheless another indication of the discrepancy between fantasy, between what advertisers claim, and what reality actually offers in suburbia today.

At the same time, there is another kind of contrast between fantasy and reality in the movie that's of a positive nature. As unlikely as this may sound, this happens first at the basketball game where Jane and her friend Angela are part of their high school's cheerleading team. Carolyn dutifully drags Lester to this event (even though, in typical teen-age fashion, Jane doesn't really want them there), and it is here that Lester's sexual re-awakening occurs. When the cheerleaders begin their performance, Lester's eyes get riveted on Angela Hayes (whose last name sounds exactly like the famed Lolita's last name—Haze—by Vladimir Nabokov). Soon the spectators as well as the other cheerleaders disappear from the screen, so that there is only Lester watching Angela and Angela apparently dancing—rather seductively at that—for Lester's sole benefit. This first short-lived fantasy is characterized by the abundance of floating rose petals that will accompany all future such fantasies. The suggestion is clear: there is something wildly romantic about this unlikely relationship between Lester and Angela, a relationship highly disapproved of by society in general to boot, yet here somehow or other not quite objectionable at all (in spite of Jane's clear embarrassment on account of it).

Both Jane and Angela become instantly cognizant of the unlikely attraction in question in the immediate aftermath of the basketball game. Jane finds her father's obvious (and clumsily disguised) attraction to Angela embarrassing, of course, whereas Angela thinks it is "sweet." She is also rather perceptive in her follow-up comment: "And I think he and your mother have not had sex in a long time." That night, in bed, as a rose petal drifts into view, we hear Lester's voice-over as he tells us that it's "as if [he had] been in a coma for about twenty years," a coma from which he is just now awakening. This happens as we see his dream-like vision of a naked Angela (her breasts and private parts being appropriately covered by rose petals) in a whole sea of roses.

These "encounters" with Angela clearly reduce Lester (even as they in some sense also revitalize him) to that awkward age which spells the beginning of our youthful search for identity when we do clumsy and even "stupid" things. Lester, for example, searches for Angela's phone number in his daughter's room (while Jane is taking a shower in an adjacent bathroom) and actually dials it, only to hang up when Angela answers the phone. Modern technology enables Angela to redial the number that has just reached her, and that's how Jane, who has come out of the shower to answer her phone, realizes—to her consternation—that her father must have dialed Angela's number, for which her additional clue is the fact that her personal phone book is open to the page where Angela's number is listed.

As the plot unfolds, each character emerges with fairly clear delineations, so that the viewers get to know them better (especially in some cases) than they know themselves and better, too (again especially in some cases), than they know each other. There are also significant thematic crossovers that require separate lines of thought in order to trace them properly. Jane's first reaction to Ricky's filming or videotaping her, for example, is one of hostility. From Angela's prior knowledge of him, we get a mixed initial picture. Jane, however, quickly picks up something that will soon lead to friendship and—eventually— love. One thing that attracts Jane to him is his unshakable confidence. As it will turn out, he has had an unpleasant past, due partly to his father's need to impose "structure and discipline."

We get a good glimpse of the kind of father-son relationship they have when the two Jims (a homosexual couple) stop by at the Fittses with a welcome-to-the-neighborhood basket. The Colonel's reaction is one of unmistakable anger at the "faggots." Ricky pretends to feel the same way about them as his father. Ricky is, of course, non-judgmental about this. In fact, he lives a double life, one of apparent respectability. His real source of income, though, is from dealing marijuana. Some people might find this objectionable, but *American Beauty* is simply accepting the fact that most people regard this as a minor crime or a venial sin.

It is at the party for realtors to which Carolyn drags Lester that Lester and Ricky emerge as, in some sense, kindred spirits. Carolyn's hero-worship of Buddy Kane, a successful realtor (and rival) is soon replete with sexual innuendo. Ricky and Lester, both outsiders at the party, connect and leave the ballroom to smoke a joint outside. When Ricky's boss comes to reprimand him for having abandoned his catering job, Ricky quits on the spot. This bold move on his part impresses Lester (who suddenly claims that Ricky has just become his hero) and it is, in fact, a thematic anticipation of Lester's own quitting later on in the story.

Lester's rebellion is reminiscent of the kind of youthful rebellion that Ricky seems quite capable of. Lester refuses to accommodate the company he works for when rather than complying with the humiliating self-study that's required of him, he writes a scathing critique of his "superiors." This amounts to quitting (he forces them to fire him), but he doesn't leave without obtaining a year's severance pay with benefits. He is a man, as he says, with nothing to lose. The theme of loss/gain is now becoming clearer. And it is one of the significant thematic threads that weaves itself into the fabric of the entire movie. His wife and daughter regard Lester a loser. He himself recognizes that suburban living has caused him to lose something vital that he aims to get back. When he loses his job, he immediately gains a new one at a fast-food restaurant appropriately named Smiley's. This takes him back, in a sense, to his youth. As he tells Ricky, who sympathizes with him over having been a hamburger flipper in his teen-age years just so he could have enough pocket money to buy eight-track tapes, Lester says that he had a good time then. He got laid a lot and his whole life was ahead of him.

Ricky and Jane become fast friends. The irony here is that Jane is attracted to a young man who is very much like her father once was and is quickly becoming again. Jane can't see through Lester's attraction to Angela, though (and is rather upset with Angela's favorable response to this, too). Angela, of course, is not what she pretends to be: a promiscuous young girl with ambitions to work her way to the top of the modeling world by letting men take advantage of her. The sexual dynamic between Lester and Angela is replicated with a big difference between the quickly emerging adulterous affair between Carolyn and her "hero," Buddy Kane, the "king" of realtors. Carolyn, in part, throws herself into this "affair" because she is disgusted with Lester's having quit his job and all that that implies. A lack of ambition is a bad thing in Carolyn's eyes. She and Buddy have a lot more in common.

The meta-cinematic theme supplied by Ricky gets us to see something significant in *American Beauty*, a kind of *ars poetica*, a kind of theory of art (as well as of life). This begins to emerge as Jane and Ricky are walking home from school on that tree-lined street we get an aerial view of from time to time. This time a funeral passes by and this prompts Ricky to tell Jane that he once saw (and filmed) a homeless woman who froze to death. What he says about this (and why he thought it was "amazing") throws light on his previous filming of a dead bird because he thought it was "beautiful."

What he tells Jane about filming the dead woman is that "When you see something like that, it's like God is looking right at you, just for a second. And if you're careful, you can look right back." Later, in his room, he shows Jane the most beautiful tape he ever made. It's a film of an empty white plastic bag blown about by the wind. This is how Ricky characterizes the video:

> It was one of those days when it's a minute away from snowing. And there is this electricity in the air, you can almost hear it, right? And this bag was just dancing with me. Like a little kid begging me to play with it. For fifteen minutes. That's the day I realized that there was this entire life behind things, and this incredibly benevolent force that wanted me to know there was no reason to be afraid. Ever. Video is a poor excuse, I know. But it helps me to remember. I need to remember. Sometimes there is so much beauty in the world I feel like I can't take it and my heart is going to cave in.

This is not only the voice of a true artist, this is also a significant statement about movies in general. They do, in fact, extend our memories. They capture life and make us see it in retrospect as if it were happening for the first time, right in front of our eyes. No wonder Jane is impressed. No wonder they kiss for the first time. Something genuine is going on between them. It's more than sex. It's understanding and (above all) the beginning of true love (if ever there was such a thing).

Two scenes follow in rapid succession, both highly telling. First the Colonel, having discovered that Ricky has been to his cabinet where he keeps special items (like the plate with the swastika on its back, a collector's item from Hitler's Germany), rushes into his room and beats him up. It is here that the Colonel accuses his son of having no respect for authority, of thinking he can do whatever he feels like doing, of not realizing that "there are rules in life," that one needs "structure and discipline."

The next scene shows Carolyn and Lester almost recapture what they once had. Lester has just bought a 1970 Pontiac Firebird (a car he had wanted to have when he was young). When Carolyn objects, Lester reminds her that once she had joy in her life. He compliments her for the way she looks and reminds her of the kind of girl she used to be. This leads to a charged atmosphere between them, but just as they are about to kiss and make up, as it were, Carolyn notices that Lester is about to spill beer on the couch (from the open bottle he happens to be holding in his hand).

This not only ruins the mood, this also spells out the conflict clearly delineated in the movie between materialism and something else, something vital, that "it" that Lester has been getting back. To Lester's angry "it's just a couch," Carolyn responds with "This is a four thousand dollar sofa upholstered in Italian silk. This is not 'just a couch.'" For Lester, though, "This isn't life. This is just stuff." The gulf between husband and wife is apparently too wide to bridge.

Lester continues to work out in the makeshift gym he sets up in his garage. He also jogs. This isn't just part of his attempt to recapture his youth. He is doing this because he has overheard Angela say that if he worked out, she would find him quite attractive. But now certain other threads begin to insinuate themselves into the plot, a whole series of misunderstood clues the Colonel uses to form erroneous hypotheses that will eventually lead to Lester's untimely and totally undeserved death.

The first of these false clues comes up when the Colonel sees Lester jog with the two Jims. He thus begins to associate Lester and his puzzling attitude (attitude puzzling to the Colonel, that is) with homosexuality. At one point he comes to snoop in Ricky's room and discovers a tape of Lester lifting weights naked in his garage. The colonel watches this with a puzzled look on his face. By now Lester has discovered Carolyn's affair with Buddy. On the final night of his life (which he announces earlier in a somewhat jocular voice-over—about a given day being the first day of the rest of one's life, except for the day on which a person dies, of course), in any case, on the final night of his life Jane has invited Angela to spend the night at their house again. The two argue about Angela's attraction to Lester. Jane pleads with Angela not to have sex with her father.

Lester, realizing that he has run out of marijuana, pages Ricky. When Ricky, in Lester's garage, rolls a joint for him, the Colonel is watching from a window in his house. The setting in Lester's garage and the Colonel's vantage point somehow combine to create the illusion that Ricky is performing fellatio on Lester. The Colonel is watching this with a dark look on his face.

In the meantime, Carolyn, on her way home with a recently acquired handgun (she has been shooting in a gallery as a result of having been "turned on" to this by Buddy), is listening to a motivational audiocassette urging her not to be a victim any more. It is raining rather heavily.

Once Ricky returns, the Colonel accuses him of being a homosexual. Ricky at first doesn't understand what his father is driving at, but once the misunderstanding is clear to him, he takes advantage of this to free himself from the Colonel's tyrannical rule over his life. Unfortunately, Ricky's false admission that he performs fellatio for money (which he makes merely for the sake of its shock value) confirms the false clue the Colonel has received earlier. The breach between father and son is final at this juncture, and Ricky immediately goes over to the Burnham house to invite Jane to go away with him to New York.

When Jane agrees, Angela objects vehemently. There is by now an unfortunate gap (due partially to misunderstandings and misperceptions) between the two girls. When Ricky tells Angela that she is "ordinary" (a significant blow to her ego, as she has repeatedly stated that this is the worst thing a person could be), Angela rushes out of the room and sits, in tears, on the stairs leading to the kitchen.

The agitated and apparently deeply anguished Colonel comes over to Lester's garage. Lester, without knowing the cause of the Colonel's dark mood, empathizes with him. After giving the Colonel the final false clue (when he remarks that the reason he doesn't mind his wife is with another man is because their marriage is "just for show, a commercial for how normal" they are), the Colonel (who has moved very close to Lester by now) kisses the stunned Lester on the lips. Lester's reaction is a gentle rebuke. He just says that the Colonel "got the wrong idea."

71

Lester now comes into the kitchen to get a beer. He hears music coming from the next room. It is Angela who has put a CD in the stereo. She admits that she has had a fight with Jane partly because she has said that Lester was sexy. The ensuing scene quickly gets rather charged, especially when Lester admits that he wants Angela, that he has wanted her since he first saw her. To Angela's question whether or not she is "ordinary," Lester's response is that she couldn't be that even if she tried.

They kiss tenderly and Lester unbuttons the quite willing Angela's blouse. They are about to commence love making when Angela blurts out that this would be her "first time." This has an immediate effect on Lester, who suddenly sees Angela not as the sexy young woman of his fantasies, but as a nervous young girl reminiscent of his own daughter. The scene now changes from one of potential coitus to a tender father-daughter moment. Lester hugs Angela and reassures her that everything will be all right. He fixes her a sandwich and asks her about Jane. He is happy to hear that Jane is in love.

When Angela goes to the bathroom, Lester is alone in the kitchen and feels apparently at peace with himself. He is sitting at the kitchen table looking at a family photo with an otherworldly smile on his face. In front of him is a vase of roses. But by now a gun has suddenly come into view behind his head, a shot rings out, and the redness of the roses is instantaneously replaced with the redness of Lester's blood.

It is not immediately clear as to who shot Lester (though the Colonel is, of course, a likely candidate), partly because we have had repeated glimpses of Carolyn in her car with a gun in her hand. When Jane and Ricky run down to the kitchen, there ensues a scene that's a thematic repetition of the one Ricky filmed of the homeless woman who froze to death. Ricky looks at Lester's lifeless eyes that, though lifeless, seem to smile and smile rather joyously back at him. This reminds us of Ricky's words about God looking at us in a situation like this and, if we are careful, how we may find ourselves looking right back at God, even if for just a second. At this point the denouement of the movie commences where rapid and short scenes intertwine as the end arrives while we seem to be in touch both with this world and, by means of Lester's agency, with the next one as well.

Lester's voice-over begins with what I see as a kind of theological conclusion to the story. "I had always heard," he says "that your entire life flashes in front of your eyes the second before you die. First of all, that one second isn't a second at all; it stretches on forever, like an ocean of time." Images from the past now alternate in black and white with the present reality as Lester recalls, with tender loving care, certain moments from his life. He remembers himself as a boy, watching falling stars. He remembers yellow leaves falling from the maple trees. He remembers his grandmother's wrinkled hands. And he remembers Janie and Carolyn.

In the meantime we get a momentary glimpse of Angela as she hears the gunshot. And we see Carolyn arrive home. She throws her gun into a hamper and then buries her face in Lester's clothes and cries. The final words of the movie are Lester's words to us from the great beyond:

> I guess [he says] I could be pretty pissed off about what happened to me, but it's hard to stay mad when there is so much beauty in the world. Sometimes I feel like I'm seeing it all at once, and it's too much, my heart fills up like a balloon that's about to burst. And then I remember to relax, and stop trying to hold unto it, and then it flows through me like rain and I can't feel anything but gratitude for every single moment of my stupid little life.

"You [says he directly to us, the viewers, now] have no idea what I am talking about, I'm sure. But don't worry. You will some day." What is particularly appealing about this theological, as it were, ending is that it is completely devoid of the kind of judgmentalism many associate with rigid, dogmatic religiosity. Lester's words are loving and reassuring. They tell us not to be afraid, just as Ricky said earlier when talking of the floating, white plastic bag that he filmed with such tender loving care and which had reminded him of a life behind things and of some benevolent force behind everything.

Lester's untimely and undeserved death may also remind us of some other words spoken by Ricky when he said, apropos of his father's not being able to realize that all of Ricky's "pocket money" couldn't have come just from odd catering jobs: "Never underestimate the power of denial." For it was the Colonel's sudden awakening to the very reality in himself of what he had denied and feared and loathed most in others throughout his entire existence up to the fateful moment that ended Lester's life while at the same time unleashing the movie's loving glimpse (from Lester's perspective) into a hereafter that none of us need fear and that all of us will eventually experience, when the time comes.

No wonder this was so popular a movie. It shows us life not just as it is (not just what we in our materialistic ways can make of it), but also as it was perhaps meant to be. It gives us hope, too, that whatever the "it" is that we (like Lester) may have lost in materialism, we may be able to regain, after all, even before we make our final way out of this world into the next. At the same time the movie is also a warning against our tendency to form false hypotheses about one another, for some of these (as, for example, the Colonel's about Lester) may lead to deadly misunderstandings that only love could have prevented from transpiring in the first place. There is, finally (this movie tells us), a better place whence even this world may look better than we have ever thought possible. What is it that we really want? What is it that we should strive for? Mistrust, suspicion, and hate? Or "faith, hope, and charity"?

Chapter Three

Hollywood Fights for Justice

1. The Verdict

[Movie Log: Released in 1982 by Twentieth Century Fox. Screenplay by David Mamet, based on a novel by Barry Reed. Directed by Sidney Lummet. Cast: Paul Newman (Frank Galvin); Charlotte Rampling (Laura Fischer); Jack Warden (Mickey Morrissey); James Mason (Edward J. Concannon); Milo O'Shea (Judge Hoyle); Lindsay Crouse (Kaitlin Costello Price); Ed Binns (Bishop Brophy); Louis J. Stadlen (Dr. Gruber); Joe Seneca (Dr. Thompson); Wesley Addy (Dr. Trowler)]

> *"If the law supposes that," said Mr. Bumble ... "the law is a[n] ass"*
> —Charles Dickens

> *Truth uncompromisingly told will always have its ragged edges*
> —Herman Melville

"The law is a[n] ass." People love to quote this famous line from Dickens. It's quite a statement, but taken out of context it may be a bit misleading. Mr. Bumble is obviously outraged when he says this. He has just indicated that it was his *wife* who committed a certain crime he has just been accused of, yet he has just been told that that still makes *him* guilty since the law assumes that a husband has control over his wife. We all know, though, that poor Mr. Bumble has been rather severely henpecked since the commencement of his holy matrimony, which is why he accuses the law of being a "bachelor." We might almost feel sorry for poor Mr. Bumble, though we should recall that it was he who was equally outraged when much earlier in the story Oliver Twist had dared to ask for more.

The quote from Melville is made of sterner stuff. It is actually an echo of the famous biblical adage that pits the letter against the spirit of the law. People interpret this as a profound insight into the dangers of going strictly by the book. The book is rigid, whereas life is fluid. The book can kill life by stopping it dead in its tracks. Ideally for a law to be just it must both

75

abide by the rules and break them. Going strictly by the rules may well compromise the truth. The truth is more than the book. Since each case is unique (no matter how much it may overlap with similar cases), each must be judged on its own merits (or demerits, as the case may be).

The story of *The Verdict* is straightforward enough, yet it subtly interacts with the points I have just outlined above. Its eventual hero, Frank Galvin, is an anti-hero in the beginning. He drinks too much. He hangs out in funeral parlors with the pathetic hope of landing personal injury cases after the fact. He plays the pinball machine in his second office, the bar (pun intended, I assume). He gets violently drunk, though the violence he perpetrates is against the furniture and the filing cabinets in his own office.

It is here that Mickey Morrisey, his friend and mentor, finds him when he brings him the case that might turn his luck around. At this point in the story turning Galvin's luck around is merely a financial matter. The case of Deborah Ann Kaye is a potential moneymaker. Every indication points toward an out-of-court settlement. Quick and easy. And easy money for Galvin. Deborah Ann Kaye came to a Catholic hospital overseen by the archdiocese of Boston to deliver a baby. She has been rendered permanently comatose by the negligence of doctors who, it is alleged, gave her the wrong anesthesia.

Behind the allegedly negligent doctors stands the powerful Catholic Church as well as the almost equally powerful law firm run by Edward J. Concannon (said to be the Prince of Darkness at one point) and his team of ambitious lawyers. Frank Galvin stands alone against what appear to be overwhelming odds. The fact that "truth" may be on his side is neither here nor there. And at this point we don't even know this for sure.

Galvin speaks to a certain Dr. Gruber who is willing to testify against all the powers that be. As he says, he is interested in doing the right thing. Isn't Galvin? Of course he would say so, but at this point Galvin's involvement in the case is still on the selfish side. The promise of easy money is still what drives him. He admits this to Bishop Brophy when he shows up in the bishop's office with snap shots he took of the bed-ridden Deborah Ann Kaye. He has counted on the lurid pictures to loosen the pocketbook of the archdiocese.

But we have seen Galvin take the pictures. And we have seen him stop suddenly and pause. His facial expression clearly indicates that this is the moment that begins to transform the ambulance chaser into something like a traditional hero. He seems to see the tragedy of it all. When he is in the bishop's office we are, I think, ready to accept Galvin's transformation, the beginning of his redemption. He speaks of the truth. It is a stroke of genius that Bishop Brophy responds with the rhetorical question "What is the truth?" A magnificent echo of the same rhetorical question raised by Pontius Pilate.

Galvin refuses the offer of the $210.000.00 (which is altogether too neatly divisible by three, making Galvin's take of a third instantly figurable). And the viewer must accept this as a momentous turning point in Galvin's development or, rather, re-birth. He is not playing games. He is not betting on a higher return for his gamble. He honestly thinks that he can win the case. He is now more interested in truth and justice than in mere money.

By now the audience's sympathy is clearly on his side. But we are not out of the woods yet. In addition to the archdiocese and the slick and well-heeled law firm that's behind the allegedly negligent doctors, Judge Hoyle is also clearly on the side of Concannon and his team of lawyers. He is so unsympathetic to Galvin that he is downright rude to him. In addition to this, Deborah Ann Kaye's sister and her husband are also disappointed and angry when Galvin doesn't take the $210,000.00. Frank Galvin is truly alone against the whole world at this point. Even his friend (and mentor) seems to disagree with his choice of action.

It is at this point that Galvin finds potential moral support in the person of Laura Fischer, a young woman he meets in his second office, the bar. She will, though, turn out to have been a kind of Judas, hired by Concannon, to be a spy in Galvin's venture at new love. By this time Galvin is soon up against more frustrations and setbacks. Dr. Gruber has disappeared. He is vacationing somewhere in the Caribbean (the suggestion is made that Concannon had gotten to him) and Judge Hoyle refuses to give Galvin a continuance.

Galvin finds a substitute in a certain Dr. Thompson, a semi-retired black doctor who hires his services to testify in medical malpractice suits. Dr. Thompson is a kind and honest man, but he is no match for Concannon and Dr. Towler, the author of a definitive book on anesthesiology. During cross-examination, aided and abetted by Judge Hoyle, Dr. Thompson has no choice but to admit that the way the question is posed to him, it doesn't appear that Dr. Towler is guilty of negligence.

At this point Galvin begins to feel that his case is hopeless. He keeps on fighting, though, breaking some rules along the way. He realizes that a certain nurse, Maureen Rooney, is keeping something back from him and is apparently protecting someone. She is bitter and lumps all lawyers together in the same sinking and stinking boat. By intercepting Maureen Rooney's mail and by checking her telephone bill, Galvin is able to track down one Kaitlin Costello Price, the admitting nurse at the time Deborah Ann Kaye was rendered comatose.

Kaitlin Costello Price lives in New York now. And is no longer a nurse. She does, however reluctantly, agree to come to Boston and testify on behalf of the plaintiff. It appears that the doctors *were* negligent. It appears that on the admittance form it was clearly stated that Deborah Ann Kaye had a meal one hour prior to being given anesthesia. Which is why she threw up in her mask and suffocated on her own vomit. It appears, too, that Dr. Towler, having had no less than five deliveries prior to coming to the aid of Deborah Ann Kaye, was too tired to look at the admittance form. Once Deborah Ann Kaye became comatose, it appears that Dr. Towler ordered Kaitlin Costello, on pain of losing her job and of never working as a nurse again, to change the numeral 1 to a 9.

The truth is now out. But the law is not cooperative. Though caught off-guard, the defense objects to Kaitlin Costello Price's testimony and manages to get it stricken from the record. The copy of the original admittance form with the 1 rather than the 9 on it isn't accepted into evidence either. This is highly ironic since in this case it is actually the original and not the copy that has been altered, though Concannon argues that the copy is not acceptable because it presupposes alteration.

We now come to the crisis of the movie, Frank Galvin's summation. It is here that the story becomes reminiscent of "The Devil and Daniel Webster." Daniel Webster, who is up against the real Prince of Darkness, wins his case because he abandons the law and appeals to the humanity of the judge and jury. Frank Galvin does the same, in a way. He speaks of our communal desire for justice. And he tells the jury that in the case at hand *they* are the law. Not the judge, not the courtroom, not the lawyers. It is up to the jury to decide what the truth is. And while the jury is out, Bishop Brophy asks a crucial question, too. When he is told how Kaitlin Costello Price's testimony has been found inadmissible, he asks "Yes, but did you *believe* her?"

It appears that the jury believed her, too. For they find for the plaintiff. And, in fact, wish to increase the money to be awarded in the case. It is here that the movie delivers its most profound insight and delineates its most telling value. The jury has clearly ignored the letter of the law by ignoring the judge's injunction against Kaitlin Costello Price's testimony. What they have done, in fact, is commit what is known as jury nullification. They went against the letter of the law in order to render its spirit triumphant. They did not let the law compromise the truth. Nor did they let the law make an ass of justice. There is an additional irony in the triumph for the plaintiff. It is that when Frank Galvin no longer fights for money, it is when he fights for truth and justice, in other words, that he wins not just truth and justice but more money than he had ever dreamed of.

The final moments of the movie round off its many poignancies. Frank Galvin is alone in his office. And his phone is ringing off the hook. Laura Fischer is trying to get through to him. She is in her apartment, lying on her bed, drinking whiskey and holding an ice pack to her aching head. Frank Galvin stares at the ringing phone in his office. He knows who is calling. But he doesn't pick up the receiver.

2. The People vs. Larry Flynt

[Movie Log: Released by Columbia Pictures in 1996. Screenplay by Scott Alexander & Larry Karaszewski. Directed by Milos Forman. Cast: Woody Harrelson (Larry Flynt); Courtney Love (Althea Leasure); Edward Norton (Alan Isaacman); Brett Harrelson (Jimmy Flynt); Donna Hanover (Ruth Carter Stapleton); James Cromwell (Charles Keating); Richard Paul (Jerry Falwell)]

We will never conquer the stupidity of fanatics and power-hungry megalomaniacs. We will never win over them. At the same time, we cannot afford to stop fighting them, for they can and will win over us.

—Milos Forman

When Milos Forman (a director well-known for such outstanding movies as *One Flew Over the Cuckoo's Nest* and *Amadeus*) first received the script, he didn't read it. What stopped him was the name "Flynt" in the title. It wasn't until further prodding (and as a courtesy to Oliver Stone) that he finally tackled the job. And then, of course, he immediately agreed to direct the movie. Many people might have the same initial reaction. Many may not want to see this movie at all, for the same negative reaction to the name alone that Milos Forman experienced, but once they overcome this reluctance, they might be in for a surprise. No, Larry Flynt will not become a lovable hero (though in the end it is impossible not to feel both compassion and admiration for him), but then neither will the likes of Jerry Falwell or Charles Keating (Larry Flynt's persistent nemeses). As Milos Forman himself stated in an interview, the real hero of the movie is the Supreme Court of the United States of America.

The movie is not trying to either defend or glorify pornography. Nor did the Supreme Court. Nor would (nor ever did) Larry Flynt himself. The best we can do is muster up a "live and let live" attitude. The fact is that there is a demand for what used to be called "girlie magazines," otherwise the likes of Larry Flynt would not become "filthy rich" (no pun intended). In a pluralistic society it is no longer possible for us to go back to being as "Danes in Denmark all day long" who know "each other well," which is Wallace Stevens's metaphor for living in a uniform culture where all think alike and share the same values (though it is doubtful that such pristine agreement could ever prevail for very long in any given culture).

In any case, the issue in *The People vs. Larry Flynt* is an important one, and what makes it a movie rather than a mere abstract argument is that the issue is intricately caught up in the personal life of a real "pornographer," the real Larry Flynt (who actually appears as a judge in the movie and who is, of course, not just a "pornographer" but, for better or worse, a complex human being as well, like all of us). We first see the character as a child in Kentucky, peddling moonshine. It is here that he espouses the idea that in America anyone can grow up to become a success. We next see him 20 years later in Cincinnati, as the owner of a sleazy joint, a poor man's version of a Playboy Club. His sole interest is in making a go of this business. His bottom line is admittedly money. And Hustler magazine gets its start from simply advertising the club (which is also called Hustler). Unlike Hugh Hefner, Larry Flynt is not interested in camouflaging the real purpose of his enterprise by dressing it up with either fancy articles or airbrushed pictures of carefully selected beauties. His "newsletter" intends to call a spade a spade (or make it look like one).

When the printer he hires insists that Larry Flynt needs to add some text to the publication in question, he reluctantly agrees to add a "joke page" to it. And it appears that part of the appeal of this publication will be, in fact, the admittedly raw representation of the female body.

The Hustler club may be an unlikely place in which to meet the love of one's life, but this is precisely what happens to Larry Flynt when he first sees Althea Leasure. They fall in love and get married and will remain "true" to each other in their own fashion for the rest of their lives till death do them part and even beyond. In spite of their sexual infidelities, they stand by each other through thick and thin, for better or worse, with admirable loyalty and steadfastness. But the nature of the club and of the publication that eventually becomes the infamous *Hustler* magazine almost from the beginning incurs the wrath of the "moral police" (particularly of one Charles Keating, a life-long foil to Larry Flynt). At the same time, the magazine becomes enormously successful and the source of great wealth for its proprietor.

The first clash with the long (and strong) arm of the law comes up relatively soon. Larry Flynt is arrested on charges of "pandering obscenity in Cincinnati and engaging in organized crime." The latter is, of course, a technicality, the kind of thing that law and order types bemoan when it gets criminals off the hook, but the kind of thing that the thought police does not object to when those innocent of the charge are nonetheless arrested. Here the movie takes a certain understandable liberty with the real story in that it implies that Alan Isaacman was Larry Flynt's lawyer throughout the history of *Hustler*'s clashes with the law. Other than this, the legal maneuvers on both sides are truthful and typical of the stance each would take. The Charles Keating types are always worried about declining morals and a bad example set for children, whereas the other side (perhaps with some justification) is always on its guard against attacks on freedom of speech. "These guys hate pornography," says Isaacman early on, "and they are going to use you [Larry Flynt] to further their national agenda."

Though the argument presented by the defense seems more convincing than that presented by the prosecutors, the judge (played by the real Larry Flynt) remains unseemly hostile. And the jury doesn't buy Isaacman's argument according to which we may not be proud of a publication like *Hustler* or a person like Larry Flynt, but we should be proud of living in a country where unpopular speech is not outlawed just because it is unpopular. If only popular speech were protected by the constitution, the freedom in question would remain a hollow commodity. The jury finds Larry Flynt guilty and the judge, angered by Larry Flynt's disrespectful behavior, sentences him to 25 years.

The conviction is not upheld and Larry Flynt is soon a free man again (and I am conscious of an irony when I use that expression, "free man," for the remainder of the story in fact deals with the various and sundry ways in which his freedom will constantly be attacked in more ways than one, including in the assassination attempt which will also deprive him of his physical freedom of movement). As will be his wont throughout his trials and tribulations, Larry Flynt immediately fights back. He puts on a big show by Americans For a Free Press (which he invents and finances himself) in which, notwithstanding the noise and glare, he raises some challenging questions. He points out, for example, that while sex is legal, depicting it is not, but while murder is illegal, depicting it is perfectly all right. Many would undoubtedly agree with the idea that while war is obscene, sex is not. The moral or thought police, on the other hand, is usually not too willing to navigate the troubled waters between the letter and the spirit of the law.

The war is now on. The authorities in Georgia arrest some newsvendors simply for selling *Hustler* magazine. When Larry Flynt gets whiff a of this, he immediately goes to Georgia, takes over a newsstand and attempts to sell a copy of *Hustler* solely for the purpose of getting arrested in order to challenge the authorities.

Whether or not the sequence that follows reflects events as they unfolded in real life is a moot question. The movie is a work of art (even if it's in part of a documentary nature) and as such it is likely to work in a plot that is itself a kind of implicit "argument" in the unfolding of the story as depicted in the movie. It is at this point that Ruth Carter Stapleton calls Larry Flynt, while he is awaiting trial for his latest arrest. This call will eventually form a kind of friendship between the "saint" and the "sinner," and it will show that not all religious people are blindly judgmental of their fellow human beings. As Ruth Carter Stapleton says at the dinner to which she has invited Larry and Althea, talk of "hellfire and damnation" is itself "almost unforgivable." Larry Flynt becomes a born-again Christian and undergoes a proper baptism in a river, in the American Baptist tradition, in the style of John the Baptist.

At the trial in Georgia Isaacman argues against "prior restraint," that is, the intimidation of newsvendors to sell a publication that has as yet not been proven unlawful. Larry Flynt's statement on the stand deserves to be quoted:

> Look, I realize it's wrong to portray women the way I have—and this is something I had to ask forgiveness for when I accepted Christ in my life. But it's not illegal! America is the greatest country in the world because anybody can do whatever they want. I think it's wrong to drink liquor, but not illegal. I think it's wrong to commit abortion, but not illegal. Our right to think for ourselves cannot be restricted!

Though they win this particular skirmish, it is here that the assassination attempt is made on Larry Flynt who, as a result, will be paralyzed from the waist down, and suffer excruciating pain for years to come, and be confined to a wheelchair for the rest of his life. The movie presents his assassin as a shadowy figure who has, unbeknownst to anyone else, been stalking Larry Flynt for quite a while. We learn nothing about who this man is. We see him as a sinister figure, but whether he is a paid-for hit man or a person acting on his own remains a mystery. I have a hunch that he is (and his real-life counterpart was) a hate-filled religious fanatic.

For years following the assassination attempt Larry Flynt needs drugs in order to deal with the pain inflicted upon him by the would-be assassin's bullets. It is at this time that Althea begins to take drugs along with Larry. She becomes a junkie and comes down with AIDS in time. When Larry undergoes an operation that frees him of pain, he stops taking drugs. Althea is unable to follow suit. It is at this point, partly due to the authorities not even trying to find his would-be assassin (who has never been found in real-life either), that Larry Flynt undertakes his private war against the United States, which is not—it appears—the land of the free and the home of the brave, after all. As he himself puts it: "They stripped me of my manhood. I have only half a life left, the half with the brain. Well, I'm gonna use it to get back at the people who did this to me." Under the circumstances, an understandable sentiment.

The remainder of the movie deals with two more major trials. In the midst of this we also witness Althea's sad and tragic demise. The first of the trials involves certain videotapes Larry Flynt has obtained involving John DeLorean who has apparently been coerced by the government into certain drug deals. When Larry Flynt refuses to identify the source of the tapes, he is charged with contempt of court. It is in this particular trial that he wears the diapers made of the American flag, on the grounds that if the United States is going to treat him like a baby, he had better behave like one. In the meantime *Hustler* magazine publishes a parody of a liquor ad in which Jerry Falwell talks of his "first time." It is alleged in this rather vulgar parody that he lost his virginity with his own mother in an outhouse.

Jerry Falwell is not amused. He decides to sue Larry Flynt, who is ready to fight with a counter suit. Jerry Falwell wins the first round here, and it is not until he states, after Althea succumbs to AIDS, that this particular disease is a plague approved of by God in order to punish those whose lifestyle is "immoral" (a really awful and mean sentiment, if you ask me) that Larry Flynt decides to take the case to the Supreme Court, if need be. The case in the Supreme Court is the climax of the story's many legal wars, which is reported in the media as "God versus the Devil. America's minister versus America's pimp." By now, however, Larry Flynt has some unlikely (perhaps not really unlikely, given the nature of the case) allies. *The New York Times* files a brief on his behalf, as does the Magazine Publishers Association as well as the American Newspaper Publishers Association. The issue? Jerry Falwell won the first round on the grounds that the parodic ad had inflicted "emotional distress" on him. Should the Supreme Court uphold the lower court's decision, it would open a veritable Pandora's box. Every public figure that would ever become the target of satire could claim "emotional distress," and this could virtually silence all public debate and critical commentary.

The argument presented by Isaacman progresses logically from the principle that "uninhibited debate and freedom of speech" have a vital interest in the United States. He also asserts that Jerry Falwell was a perfect candidate for the kind of parody *Hustler* magazine inflicted on him in that he has consistently spoken out against everything the magazine stood for and thus the magazine had every right to imply that he was full of "B.S." (This abbreviation is actually used in Isaacman's speech.) The difference between claiming (admittedly parodically) that Jerry Falwell had sex with his mother in an outhouse and that George Washington is "being led by a donkey on an ass" (from an Editorial Cartoon of 200 years ago) is "a matter of taste—not law." To deny this would ultimately amount to no more than to "allow the punishment of unpopular speech."

The final scenes of the movie bring with them a triumph and a heart-rending last look at Larry Flynt. The triumph is the verdict, read to Larry Flynt by Alan Isaacman over the phone. This is what the Supreme Court has unanimously decided:

> At the heart of the First Amendment is the recognition of the fundamental importance of the free flow of ideas. The freedom to speak one's mind is not only an aspect of individual liberty, but essential to the quest for truth and the vitality of society as a whole. In the world of debate about public affairs, many things done with motives that are less than admirable are protected by the First Amendment. The fact that society may find speech offensive is not a sufficient reason to suppress it.

This restores Larry Flynt's faith in the United States. But it cannot undo the untimely and horrible death to which his beloved Althea had succumbed. Our last view of Larry is his watching Althea (and himself) on a crude home movie on television, as he lies in bed, unable to move his legs. Tears fill his eyes as he watches the images on the screen in the shadowy twilight of a black and white video. As the credits roll, we get statements of update about some of the major players in this drama. Nothing new here, except with respect to Charles Keating, Larry Flynt's self-righteous and mortal enemy. We are told that he has been "convicted of 72 counts of racketeering, fraud, and conspiracy. His trials revealed his actions cost taxpayers over 2 billion dollars." Sometimes members of the moral police may not be moral at all, which is one of the lessons it is important to take to heart from a movie such as *The People vs. Larry Flynt*.

I want to end this discussion by saying a few more words about Milos Forman and why he so readily took on this enterprise, once he got past his own admitted prejudice against the name "Flynt" itself. In an interview published in the Newmarket Press edition of the shooting script, he talks of the Nazis and Communists who also began their successful suppression of ideas by first going after the "perverts." Once they gained power, though, it was easy for them to include more and more under this label, so that anyone who disagreed with certain government policies might easily be silenced on the grounds of "perversion." It is altogether too easy to think that those who don't think exactly the way we do have somehow or other become perverted. This reminds me of one of Emerson's brilliant observations in "Self-Reliance," where he says that people tend to "think that your rejection of popular standards is a rejection of all standards." Oppressive governments are, of course, just as likely to think this as the populace. We must always stay on guard against those who, according to the popular expression, are always willing to throw the baby out with the bathwater. There is no point in siding with the letter of the law when it attempts to kill the very spirit that gave it life in the first place.

3. Nuts

[Movie Log: Released in 1987 by Warner Bros. Screenplay by Tom Topor, Darryl Ponicsan, and Alvin Sargent (Based on the play by Tom Topor). Directed by Martin Ritt. Cast: Barbra Streisand (Claudia Draper); Richard Dreyfuss (Aaron Levinsky); Maureen Stapleton (Rose Kirk); Karl Malden (Arthur Kirk); Eli Wallach (Dr. Herbert A. Morrison); Robert Webber (Francis MacMillan); James Whitmore (Judge Stanley Murdoch); Leslie Nielsen (Allen Green)]

> Gabriela: "You believe everything the authorities tell you?"
> Kafka: "I have no reason to doubt."
> Gabriela: "They are the authorities. That's reason enough."
> —Stephen Soderbergh, *Kafka* (1991)

Quite simply *Nuts* is about a woman fighting to be heard, fighting for the right to speak in her own right, in her own voice, fighting for the right to have a voice of her own. And for this the "authorities" think of her as mentally disturbed, as a person who needs psychiatric care, as a person who belongs in a hospital rather than in jail (or, eventually, in prison). It so happens that she is innocent (certainly until proven guilty). If she goes along with the "authorities," her freedom (as an innocent person) is at stake. So she is quite right to fight for her rights. Her name is Claudia Draper and she is charged with manslaughter in the first degree.

The movie opens with a scene in a crowded jail cell, full of women. When those who are to appear in court are called, the name Kirk is used,

Claudia's "maiden" name by virtue of her stepfather. Right at the outset, then, she is—in a sense—denied use of her own name. Her parents, stepfather and mother, show up with an expensive (and therefore said to be good) lawyer for her defense. The prosecutor claims that she is not competent to stand trial. Hearing this Claudia interrupts the proceedings (a thing she will do frequently whenever the authorities are arrogantly assuming that they are acting in her own best interest without asking for her permission to do so). When her lawyer tells the judge that she "won't listen," and when he tells her that what they are doing is what they feel is best for her, her response is to say that she didn't grant them any such permission, that she is innocent. "That's not the issue," says the lawyer. The only thing that should matter is *not* the issue? No wonder Claudia Draper is mad!

She punches her lawyer in the nose (perhaps breaking it in the process) right there in the courtroom, at the time of her preliminary hearing. Aaron Levinsky, the lawyer the court will appoint to defend her, has been watching the proceedings with a certain degree of interest. Guards carry her away against her will, to the psychiatric ward of the jail. From the very beginning Mr. Levinsky acts in her true behalf. He moves to controvert the motion of incompetence. He wants to consult with Claudia Draper, to make sure he does what *she* wants. He will, in fact, prove to be the only person who will truly try to represent *her* and not what others think is good for her. In the corridor Claudia's stepfather confronts the lawyer, displeased with the motion to controvert. He, Arthur Kirk, also reiterates what is almost a slogan already, that she belongs in a hospital and not in prison. Rose Kirk sends her "love" by way of Mr. Levinsky. As we will soon learn, this is a "loaded" word.

Just prior to meeting with Claudia, Mr. Levinsky runs into Dr. Morrison, one of two psychiatrists who has already issued a statement that Claudia Draper is not competent to stand trial. When Levinsky wants to know whether she is "crazy" or not, the doctor's response is that "crazy is a word" he "does not like." This obfuscation is, of course, part and parcel of a certain rhetoric that prefers scientific terms with which to label others (even those, as it turns out at times, who need no labels at all). As Claudia follows the other doctor (the one who speaks with a heavy Spanish accent) through the corridors for the consultation with Mr. Levinsky, we get the second flashback in the movie. We see Claudia follow the waiter in a restaurant to the table where a certain Allen Green (the man she will be charged of having killed) is waiting for her. (The first flashback in the movie occurs almost in the opening sequence, when a group of women are led by the men's cells on the way to the courtroom. Here the flashback is to a bar where men stand around checking out the women—these scenes are preliminary images that identify Claudia Draper's profession, the oldest in the world. She is a prostitute. Not a streetwalker, but an expensive call girl.)

At the very beginning of their first consultation Claudia is highly mistrustful of Aaron Levinsky. She wants to know what kind of "show" she needs to put on, for it doesn't seem to her that she can ever get a fair trial without putting on some kind of "show." When she hears that her mother sends her "love," she becomes angry and accuses Levinsky of working for "them." Levinsky tells her that if she chooses to cooperate with him, things might go her way. Otherwise he will just sign the relevant papers that will put her away. Claudia relents (she clearly begins to sense that this lawyer is not like all the others), but she insists that no more "shrinks" be brought into the picture. A mistake from Levinsky's point of view as two "shrinks" have already testified that Claudia Draper is not competent to stand trial. To controvert their testimony another "shrink" would be required. Claudia offers that she herself should be her own "case." It seems that everyone wants her to behave "like a good little girl," overlooking the fact that she is an adult, quite capable of taking care of herself. She tells Levinsky that she is willing to risk a trial (if found guilty she stands to spend time in prison), because the alternative is to become the ward, as it were, of the psychiatric establishment and to stay hospitalized, as she puts it, till she is old enough to collect Social Security.

When Levinsky next runs into Mr. MacMillan, the prosecuting attorney, he informs the latter that he is going to defend Claudia Draper at the competency hearing. "A big mistake," says Mr. MacMillan, the "girl is sick." This demotion, as it were, from "woman" to "girl" should not escape us. Levinsky's response is to assert Claudia's right to have her day in court. The issue of "trust" comes up again the next time Claudia is called into Dr. Morrison's office. She does not trust him because he wants to put her away. When she is told that she is angry, she says (and rightly so) that she has a lot to be angry about. Dr. Morrison feels that she needs treatment in order to learn to control herself. What he means by this, of course, is that she should behave "like a good little girl" and go along with whatever the "authorities" think is the right thing. When she tells the doctor that she knows more about him than he knows about her, she means (of course) that she is familiar with the male psyche (and male sexuality), as a result of her own "professional" experience.

In the meantime Mr. Levinsky has gotten permission to go to her apartment (his intention is to bring Claudia clothes to wear at the competency hearing). This is, of course, also the scene of the crime (there is a blood stain on the bathroom floor and the chalk drawing, which indicates the position of the body of the slain man, Allen Green). But Levinsky sees other things here as well. Family photos and books. At one point we clearly see books by Lawrence Durrell (the volumes of his famous *Alexandria Quartet*). When he next comes to the psychiatric ward (bringing Claudia a pastrami sandwich as well as her clothes), he finds her sitting at a table in the company of a woman doctor who doesn't think that she needs to be committed. When this doctor turns out to be a patient at the ward, Levinsky gets the joke (which, in a way, is no joke at all, as the pretend doctor's advice may well be better than the advice offered by the bona fide professionals). When Claudia finds out that Mr. Levinsky has been to her apartment, she gets angry, for she hasn't given him permission to do this. She feels "invaded." Levinsky apologizes. He is truly sorry he didn't think he had time to ask her for permission. He just wanted her to wear "sane" clothes at the upcoming competency hearing.

It is at this point that we get a flashback to the manslaughter. The connecting link is mention of Claudia's underwear ("I decide who sees my underwear," she says to Levinsky). We suddenly see Allen Green handling Claudia's sexy underwear in her apartment. As far as Claudia is concerned, the session is over. But Mr. Green doesn't want to leave. He begins to draw water for a bath and says that he likes to "bathe girls." (Why this particular line makes Claudia angry will be revealed in due course). He quickly becomes violent with her and it is during this struggle, while he is on top of her in the bathroom, that she picks up a piece of shattered glass (or mirror) and stabs him in the throat with it. (As she will later say, with a bit of a play on words, the case was really a question of "womanslaughter," only she "finished first"—an indication that she was clearly defending herself). The flashback ends as Claudia suddenly wakes up from a nightmare, perhaps "allegorizing" the fact that one man's controlling violence has landed her in the trouble she is in, against her will.

When the competency hearing commences Mr. Levinsky's first move is to state that Claudia Draper has refused a new psychiatric evaluation against his advice. She jokes with him about "covering his ass," an indication that she has begun to trust him. The prosecutor's first witness is, of course, Dr. Morrison who calls Claudia's conviction that people are trying to put her away a form of paranoia (which should strike us as a rather bizarre twisting of the truth—the authorities *are* trying to put her away). Mr. Levinsky's cross-examination quickly shows us that it is, in fact, Dr. Morrison who has been hostile to Claudia Draper simply because she challenged his authority. Dr. Morrison angrily recites a whole litany of "charges," that Claudia comes from a broken home and a broken marriage, and that her prostitution and homicidal rage all point to serious psychological problems. When Mr. Levinsky objects, Judge Stanley Murdoch says that he knows the law, too, and that Mr. Levinsky should "trust" him. (This issue of "trust" keeps coming up in the movie, which is—ultimately—precisely about that, who should we trust? When are the "authorities" truly allowing us to be who we are rather than who they want to see us as?)

Claudia doesn't want to see her mother testify. But Rose Kirk does testify after a short recess and in her testimony relates how Claudia became a problematic child at a certain point in her development. At one point, around the age of 16 (by which time she had also smoked marijuana and had also been promiscuous) she once brandished a pair of scissors as a weapon against her parents. (During this testimony we get a quick flashback to Claudia as a very young girl sitting on her bed and crying—we see her mother close the door to her room without trying to determine the reason for Claudia's tears.) When Mr. MacMillan asks Rose Kirk whether she would like to see Claudia get psychiatric help, Claudia disrupts the proceedings (a thing she does often). What difference does it make what her mother thinks? She (Claudia) is a grown-up. When she insists that Levinsky not cross-examine her mother (in order to discredit her testimony), he whispers, "maybe you are crazy," under his breath.

With Mr. Kirk's testimony things begin to change and unravel in unexpected ways. We also get several flashbacks here which clearly indicate that Claudia's stepfather had sexually abused her when she was a young girl (and that some of the abuse took place in their bathroom, which explains why Claudia got angry when Mr. Green wanted to "bathe" her). It is almost impossible to pinpoint the precise moment at which Mr.

Levinsky begins to "smell a rat," but at one point "I bathed her" slips into Mr. Kirk's testimony about his carrying out what he conceived of as his "fatherly duties." When questioned about how long this "bathing" her had been going on, Claudia finally blurts out that it went on until she was 16. A stunned silence falls upon the courtroom. Even the judge clearly realizes the gravity of the situation.

It would, however, be a mistake to think that this is one of those victim stories. Though these childhood experiences clearly traumatized Claudia when she was young, it is also clear that she has overcome them. Levinsky gets angry with Dr. Morrison when at this point he sedates her. Levinsky doesn't want her "drugged," like a "zombie." There is a tender scene when Aaron comes to see her as she is lying abed in her sedated state. It is clear that there is a real human connection between lawyer and client, so that the words "lawyer" and "client" could easily be replaced by just loving friends. When Claudia's turn comes to finally testify in her own behalf, she rejects the judge's suggestion that she stay at her table. She insists on taking the stand, the same as everybody else. To the question whether she understands the charges against her, she shows not only that she is fully aware of the law, but also the danger possibly facing her if she agrees to psychiatric treatment. They could possibly keep her hospitalized for decades without a trial. She wants to risk a trial (even if there is the potential that she might be found guilty).

During cross-examination the prosecutor does his best to discredit her, on the grounds of her failed marriage, on the grounds of an abortion she once had (she doesn't "believe in childhood," as she puts the reason for this), on the grounds of the source of her income (gifts, including cash, from men for certain favors rendered). They skirt around the issue of prostitution and the reason why Claudia didn't turn to her parents for financial help until she finally states that "it hurts less to sell yourself to strangers." The question of trust emerges once again, and (given this) Claudia's responses are eminently reasonable: she doesn't trust those who can hurt her. When the question of her competency comes up, she raises the question of Dr. Morrison's competency. "What if he is just an asshole with the power to lock me up? What if he is just an asshole with power?" What indeed.

To the question of love, Claudia's response is equally telling. Of course her mother loves her! But what does that mean? "Sometimes people love you so much their love is like a God damn gun that keeps firing into your head." To her mother's insistence that she "didn't know," Claudia's response is that she "didn't want to know." In fact, in retrospect, Claudia's stepfather's strong insistence that what Claudia needs is hospitalization and psychiatric care may suddenly seem something in the nature of a cover-up. In spite of all these very reasonable and clear indications that Claudia is not only fully competent but also a highly intelligent adult, Dr. Morrison proves incapable of changing his opinion. When she returns to her table, Levinsky congratulates her for having told the truth and also tells her that he, at least, "heard" it, too. In a final outburst Claudia insists on not wanting to be a "picture" in other people's heads. That she cannot be turned into a "nut" no matter who signs how many papers to that effect. In his summation Mr. Levinsky admits that his client is a "real pain in the ass," but that the authorities shouldn't confuse her behavior with her capacity to stand trial. As it turns out, the judge will have heard the truth as well as Claudia's mother. Just prior to the judge's returning from his chambers we witness a tender scene, a mother-daughter hug that culminates in an emotional closure long overdue.

When the judge returns with a favorable verdict, she happily walks out of the courtroom and our last glimpses of her are on one of Manhattan's crowded avenues, perhaps Fifth Avenue. As the credits roll we are informed that Mr. Levinsky was her defending attorney at her trial and that she was acquitted. The feeling the movie leaves behind is that justice has triumphed. But it didn't come without a struggle as well as without some rather significant insights. Namely, that families can be dysfunctional and even harmful in unexpected ways. That "life," as Claudia tells Dr. Morrison early on, "has no order." That we must do the best we can, at times against incredible odds. That the authorities are not automatically the "good guys," no matter how much they try to convince themselves (or us) of this. Perhaps the final question that raises itself as we continue to think about this movie is this: why is it so difficult to hear the other person, in this case Claudia? Why do parents and other "authority" figures assume that they know what is best for us? Have they walked the proverbial mile in our shoes?

4. Erin Brockovich

[Movie Log: Released in 2000 by Universal Pictures and Columbia Pictures. Screenplay by Susannah Grant. Directed by Stephen Soderbergh. Cast: Julia Roberts (Erin Brockovich); Albert Finney (Ed Masry); Aaron Eckhart (George); Scotty Leavenworth (Matthew); Gemmenne de la Peña (Katie); Marg Helgenberger (Donna Jensen); Cherry Jones (Pamela Duncan); Peter Coyote (Kurt Potter); Veanne Cox (Theresa Dallavale); Erin Brockovich-Ellis (Waitress)]

> *Oh, what a tangled web we weave,*
> *When first we practice to deceive!*
> —Sir Walter Scott

A "triumph of the human spirit" was a popular expression in the 1970s. It fits *Erin Brockovich* like a glove. The person as well as the movie. A twice-divorced mother of three, down and out on her luck, Erin is without a job and without prospects in the beginning. We first see her in a doctor's office bravely undergoing an interview for a job for which she is not officially qualified (but which she could probably learn quickly enough, given half a chance). Leaving the doctor's office in disappointment, she finds a parking ticket under the windshield wiper of her car. And no sooner does she drive off than a Jaguar sideswipes her, leaving her with an injured neck due to whiplash.

Ed Masry, the lawyer she hires, has every confidence that she will win the case against the doctor whose car hit hers, but this turns out not to be the case. The lawyer for the defense manages to convince the jury that Erin is somehow using this accident (which, by implication, she deliberately staged) as a source of easy money. The whole thing rightly demoralizes Erin, but her spirit is undaunted. In fact, her brassy, no-nonsense attitude quickly manifests itself when she asks Ed Masry whether they are taught how to apologize in law school, because he clearly "sucks at it."

To make matters worse, she loses her babysitter as well. In the restaurant where she takes her kids (because there is nothing really to eat at home), the kids order food, but she can only afford a cup of coffee, while she bravely tells her children that she is still stuffed as her lawyer took her out to lunch after the trial to celebrate. The waitress who waits on them is none other than the real Erin Brockovich. This adds a special touch to the movie. It is certainly a pleasure to see her in this role, brief as her performance is. (I think, though I am not entirely sure about this, that the man sitting behind Erin in the restaurant is the real Ed Masry himself, which would add a further special touch to the movie as a whole.)

Erin may dress like a hooker and talk like a sailor (though these days few people would blush), but her heart is like an angel's and her mind like a rocket scientist's, certainly a diamond in the rough. Her life has taught her many lessons in the proverbial school of hard knocks, and she has learned them well, which is (in part) why she takes no chances when it comes to using a sharp tongue (she is certainly not a push-over or a doormat). She just about hires herself at Ed Masry's office. And when Ed confronts her, in utter bewilderment, she tells him that he needs her, else the office would return calls and would not be in general as inefficient as it appears to be.

The exchange between Erin and Ed is the first sign of real humanity operating between them. She tells him, in her usual brash tone of voice, that she is not leaving the office without a job, but then she whispers to him not to make her beg. If it doesn't work out, she says, he can always fire her. This is the first positive thing that happens to her in the story up to this point. But the evening of the same day finds her with yet another unpleasant confrontation.

Erin has just put the kids to bed when she is alarmed by a loud noise; a motorcycle is being revved up. Not being the kind who is easily intimidated, Erin confronts the man with her customary "charm" (that language again, which used to make sailors blush). First impressions are not always accurate, though. George turns out to be a nice guy, though Erin is taking no chances. When he wants her number, first she gives him quite a few, like the ages of her children, the 16 dollars in her bank account, and (finally) her phone number, which she predicts George is going to call zero times because of all Erin's other numbers.

This turns out not to be the case. When Erin finds that her babysitter's house is empty and her own house is without her children, she is just about to panic when she discovers them happily attending a spontaneous picnic next door, in George's backyard. Erin is alarmed by this turn of events, but she begins to see George as a real person and a possibly valuable friend. Of course, the playful exchange of not being interested in each other in anything like a romantic way ("This isn't going to get you laid, you know," she tells him) is not something the viewer may take seriously. Sometimes things are not exactly what we say they are.

At the office the "girls" are not at all friendly with Erin. When Ed wants to know why she is not out to lunch with them, she says that she is apparently "not the right kind." Words about the "dress code" come up here, but Erin defends (in her usual no-nonsense manner) her choice of fashion (and even suggests that Ed might rethink the kind of ties he wears). It is at this point in the story that the "real" story begins, Erin Brockovich's heroic fight against a huge corporation. But the beginning is rather innocuous at first: she is given some files in a pro-bono real estate case. Erin is puzzled when she finds "medical records and blood samples" among the files. They don't seem to fit. When Anna, one of her co-workers, refuses to assist her, she goes to Ed to see if she might "investigate" this further. Ed happens to be on the phone at the time and is hardly paying any attention to her. He gives her the go-ahead rather absent-mindedly and Erin takes off.

Like a real pro, like an independent agent, in fact, Erin goes to explore the thing that puzzles her. She visits Donna Jensen in Hinkley, California, to see why her medical bills have been "mixed up" with the files in which PG&E (the Pacific Gas & Electric Company) has placed offers to buy her house. (A remarkable and characteristic exchange takes place here: to Donna's question whether Erin is a lawyer, she responds with her usual aplomb, "Hell, no. I hate lawyers. I just work for them.") It is to Erin's credit that she quickly smells a rat. Why would the power company be paying for medical bills? And what has "chromium" in the water got to do with it?

Erin wastes no time. She goes to UCLA where she talks to a cooperative professor who informs her that there is a kind of chromium ("chrom 6" or "hexavalent chromium"), which is highly toxic and which power companies use as a rust inhibitor. Once more Erin wastes no time. She immediately goes to the Water Board where she quickly finds among the files for Hinkley a "Clean-up and Abatement Order" issued by the water board to PG&E. She even has the presence of mind to make Xerox copies of certain of these files. She has been working hard, on her own initiative to boot, and has stumbled upon something potentially big. Yet the next time she shows up at her office, she finds that she has been fired. The reason? She hasn't been showing up for work. We know that she has been working hard and perhaps even brilliantly, but what do bosses know at times? They think conventionally and are victimized by mere appearances (as Ed tells her later, he assumed that she was out there having fun. Why? Because she looks like the type who has a lot of fun).

In the next sequence we find out a great deal about Erin, about just what kind of woman she really is underneath that tough exterior of hers. She tells George that she was once a beauty queen (Miss Wichita) and that she had high hopes then, wanted to do something with her life, wanted to make the world a better place, wanted to bring about "an end to world hunger" and contribute "to the creation of a peaceful earth for every man, woman, and child." Of course, she says much of this with tongue-in-cheek, but her sincerity and good will also shine through, though even in the days of her reign she had realized the hopelessness of such ideals, for she knew that once she got through with opening a lot of supermarkets, there wasn't going to be much time left for the fulfillment of her idealistic dreams.

In the meantime Ed gets a call from the professor from UCLA and realizes that Erin has been up to something potentially important. He comes to call on her at her home to let her know about the call. "Isn't it funny," says Erin, "how some people go out of their way to help people while others just fire them." Ed is, of course, willing to rehire her now and, once more, it is to Erin's credit that she uses this opportunity to get a 10 percent raise and benefits. It is also to her credit that she realizes that she has assets that are rather obvious. When Ed wants to know why she thinks she can just get back to the Water Board and make more copies of more relevant documents, her simply response is "They're called boobs, Ed."

It is not until Erin returns to the Jensen house that Donna slowly realizes that the power company has lied to them, that the chromium in their water is highly toxic and poisonous. Once the truth is out, Donna immediately orders her children out of the pool. And once the power company knows that something is up, they immediately send a representative with the telling last name of Foil. It is from Mr. Foil that they learn just how rich the company in question is. This is both good and bad, of course, in that the richer the company, the more the potential payoff, but also the more it can afford to use all sorts of tactics to delay an outcome. Erin now throws herself whole-heartedly into the work necessary to move the case forward. So much so that her son, Matthew, begins to resent her frequent absences from home. George steps in as a husband-father substitute, but in time even he will begin to resent Erin's devotion to the cause she so willingly and enthusiastically espouses.

Erin's no-nonsense and surprisingly commonsensical interventions here and there are nothing short of amazing. When, for example, she and Ed are talking with several families about a possible lawsuit and when these people find out that Ed would take 40 percent of whatever monies they might win, it is Erin who makes them see that Ed is taking a risk, too, in that if they don't win anything, he gets nothing at all for all the time and expense he will have put into the case. It is also Erin who makes Ed see that staying for a cup of coffee after the business part of their visit is over is a good and friendly thing to do. And it is to Ed's credit that he responds positively to Erin's humanizing suggestions.

But Erin does more than "merely" humanize her boss. She is also the one who fires him up to do this job, to undertake the case against all odds. Ed, the experienced lawyer who has worked hard all his life and who was looking forward to an early retirement, is rather discouraged by the ever-growing complexity of the case. He knows what a powerful company is capable of in terms of obstacles, in terms of dragging the case out for years and years. It is Erin who is certain that they must continue with the fight, that the powerful company in question lied, that it knowingly misled the people of Hinkley. It is Erin who says to Ed, "Don't you ever just know?" She admits that she doesn't know all the logistics, but she says—nay shouts—her certain knowledge of the "difference ... BETWEEN RIGHT AND WRONG!" (Capitals in screenplay).

True to her word, Erin goes out into the field to collect samples. She works hard and she works furiously, because she believes in her cause, and rightly so. Even a threatening phone call is powerless to daunt her resolve to go on. When George suggests that she might be out of her league here, her response is to say that that's exactly what PG&E wants her to think. It is also to her credit that she traces the source of the call back to the man at the Water Board, as he was the only one aware of her middle name (which she uses when she first signs in to examine documents there).

The first real break for Masry & Vititoe comes at a point in the story where Erin herself realizes that things can be very risky indeed. A judge can stop their "cause of action," should the judge accept PG&E's "demurs" against "the four hundred or so plaintiffs" Ed will take before him or her. In which case PG&E would go scot-free and no one would get a penny. Luckily the judge strikes the motions and demurs submitted by PG&E and gives Masry and Vititoe the go-ahead for a trial.

This first triumph notwithstanding, all this work begins to take more and more of a toll on Erin's personal life. In time it isn't just her son Matthew but George, too, who feels neglected. And Erin realizes what has been at stake all along as well, when it was George, for example, who had to report to her the fact that her little girl, her youngest child, had uttered her first word. Nine months have now gone by and George is actually ready to call it quits. Either Erin quits this job or he will quit Erin. But George is asking too much. This isn't just a job for Erin, for the first time in her life people respect her, and for the first time in her life she is not willing to bend her will to what the man in her life may want. George is right in telling her that he has been different than her ex husbands, but to really prove this Erin simply asks him to just "stay" on with her. But by this time George feels unwanted. He also feels that Erin can now afford to hire a babysitter so he is no longer really needed. Of course he overlooks the emotional need Erin has for him, but his feelings are hurt at the moment and he does walk out on her (for the time being).

Erin remains undaunted. We see this clearly when she sums up the importance of the case against PG&E with passion when she tells Pamela Duncan (one of the plaintiffs originally hostile to her): "See, the thing is ... it doesn't matter if you win lose or draw here. You were lied to. You're sick, your kids are sick because of those lies, if for no other reason, you all have to come together to stand up in a courtroom and say that." By this time, though, the case is so big, with so many litigants involved, that Ed feels it necessary to enlist the services of an expert in such cases, one Kurt Potter. Erin now becomes jealous of her work. When Potter's assistant, Theresa Dallavale, suggests that they need to do more work on Erin's files, Erin blows her top and quickly proves that there is nothing more to be added to her work, that it is complete. She is rather unpleasant to poor Theresa in her diatribe and the latter realizes that she has bitten off much more than she can chew when she suggested that Erin's files might be in need of more work.

But Erin soon feels that she is up against more than Theresa. She feels that Ed is taking the whole thing away from her. She has a bad cold at this moment and is furious with Ed for meeting with Kurt Potter behind her back, as it were. When Ed accuses her of being too "emotional" and "erratic" and of making the whole thing "too personal," Erin's response is to assert her personal involvement. "That's my work in there," she says, "My sweat, my time away from my kids. If that's not personal, I don't know what is." Ed wants her to go home at this point and get well. He needs her, he says. The case needs her. But Ed has not told this to Kurt Potter and Theresa Dallavale, which doesn't sit well with Erin at all.

The next major obstacle is twofold: they need to convince the plaintiffs that "binding arbitration" (which is not unlike a trial but without a jury) is the best way to win the case, but to make this work, they need all the participants to sign up, for which they need to do a lot of legwork real fast. Erin is, once again, up to the task. By this time even Matthew comes to see the value in the work her mother has been doing. He picks up a file and reads about a young girl who is the same age as he is and who is "one of the sick people," and suddenly realizes what has really been at stake here all along.

The clincher for the case is the revelation that PG&E has ordered a certain worker to destroy documents. The information comes from a former employee of the power company, and it is of vital importance in that it establishes a link between the company's main office in San Francisco and the local branch in Hinkley. By this time it is also clear that Erin can learn from Ed, too. It is Ed who tells her not to scare off the former employee by bombarding him with a lot of questions. Ed says that she should just let him talk and tell his story his own way. Of course he also reminds Erin that she is good at this, because if it weren't for her, Ed would be in Palm Springs by this time.

The movie does not take us to the courtroom in the end. Though that's what the whole case has been leading up to, the movie concentrates on the background work that Erin, especially Erin, has been able to accomplish. We find out about the outcome when Erin takes George with her to Donna Jensen's house in order to show him what he has been helping her with. She tells Donna that the judge has come up with a number, that they were awarded 333 million dollars all told and that Donna's family's share of this is five million. Donna is overwhelmed and when she hugs Erin out of infinite gratitude, the latter looks over her shoulder at George and smiles with tears in her eyes. This is what this case has been all about: to win for the people who were lied to and rendered sick by a powerful but indifferent and greedy company.

The final scene in the movie is an absolute delight. Erin is sitting in her office, at work on a new case. Ed receives her bonus check and takes it to her, but tells her that the sum is not what they had previously discussed. Ed is full of mischief at the moment, knowing full well how Erin is going to react. Indeed she gives him quite an earful. She accuses Ed of using big words he doesn't understand, like "trust," and that as a lawyer all he can do is complicate things that aren't complicated to begin with. She is outraged at the way her work is undervalued "in this firm." In the meantime Ed has handed her the check the figure on which is two million dollars. Once Erin notices the amount, she is struck absolutely speechless, probably for the first time in her life. Mischievous Ed, in a sense, has the last word when he re-plays for her her own first repartee thrown at him. He asks her whether they "teach beauty queens to apologize," because Erin "suck[s] at it."

Quite a triumph for the human spirit indeed. What this true story reveals is that nothing is impossible. That even a single person, a divorced mother of three, can accomplish great things and bring about a splendid victory for a just cause. And it is to the real Erin Brockovich-Ellis's credit that in a statement after the release of the movie she said: "I don't see [that] this movie is about me. Never have. And it's not about me. I happen to be a vehicle that's getting the message out about a much greater story and a much greater issue that impacts all of us." We can learn a great deal from her. Would that we were all capable of taking her lesson to heart: the one-time beauty queen's dream for the "creation of a peaceful earth for every man, woman, and child," which suddenly no longer seems like such an impossibility.

Chapter Four

Hollywood Makes a Difference

1. Amadeus

[Movie Log: Released in 1984 by The Saul Zaentz Company. Screenplay by Peter Shaffer, based on his own play. Directed by Milos Forman. Cast: Tom Hulce (Wolfgang Amadeus Mozart); F. Murray Abraham (Antonio Salieri); Elizabeth Berridge (Constanze Mozart); Roy Dotrice (Leopold Mozart); Jeffrey Jones (Emperor Joseph II); Charles Kay (Count Orsini-Rosenberg); Jonathan Moore (Baron Van Swieten); Patrick Hines (Kappelmeister Bonno); Simon Callow (Emanuel Schikaneder)]

> *But it's the truth even if it didn't happen.*
> —Ken Kesey, *One Flew Over the Cuckoo's Nest*

Neither the play nor the movie tells us the factual truth about Mozart. But both tell us a significant truth just the same (and, for all we know, the truth they tell us may be closer to what actually happened than anyone can tell for sure). A life, like history itself, is remembered, recovered, and invented. The life itself, once it's over, is gone forever; only the memories, the documents, the speculations remain. It is out of these that both historians and poets weave the texts that attempt to tell us the "truth." If they are honest and work as consciously free of prejudices and preconceived notions as humanly possible, the "truth" we get is something we can trust and believe to a large extent. There is no perfect or absolute truth, not for us, not on this earth. But that doesn't mean that what we have should be dismissed on that ground.

An artist, like Peter Shaffer, has a legitimate recourse to poetic license. The story that *Amadeus* tells is, in part, the story of the historic Mozart, but it is also just a story, a work of art, which (like all works of art) presents us with an argument (in the philosophical sense) and a theme. The real story is actually there, lurking behind all speculations (all the myths and legends, if you will). Shortly after Mozart died (at the untimely age of 35), for example, the story was told that he had a pauper's funeral and was interred in a common, unmarked grave. The fact is that at the time

Steven C. Scheer

Mozart died, funerals were, by royal decree, to be simple affairs. Even common graves were not uncommon. But, as Peter Gay, the author of Mozart's biography in the Penguin Lives Series remarks, "there is something satisfying about the sorry spectacle of the genius neglected, something romantic about the contrast between the lonely artist and the philistine world in which he is forced to live, and die."

It is precisely this aspect, this "something romantic," that Peter Shaffer's version of Mozart's life picks up and explores. The movie is more "realistic" than the play. In the movie Salieri "confesses" to a priest; in the play he conjures himself up from the past, as it were, and then "confesses" to the audience in the theater. This, in a sense, is more imaginative than the movie version, and at the very end of the play there is a moment (which I found rather startling and disturbing, too) when the audience almost identifies and agrees with Salieri, the "Patron Saint of Mediocrities." In the movie version this plays differently. Here Salieri blesses the inmates of the insane asylum rather than "us." The movie nevertheless remains the story, perhaps even the allegory, of how excellence fares in a world populated mostly by "mediocrities," though perhaps that isn't the right word in that it conjures up the ghost of elitism. The story is more like the romantic unfolding of a paradox. At the heart of it is a contest between Salieri and God, reminiscent of the conflict between Satan and the Creator in the Book of Job. But I am getting ahead of the story, so let's take a look at what happens and how things evolve.

Old Salieri attempts to cut his own throat even as he asks Mozart's forgiveness for having killed him. As he is carried to the hospital on a stretcher we see people dancing to Mozart's music in a stately ballroom. When the priest comes to visit him in his room in the insane asylum, Salieri is sitting by a small forte-piano playing some of his own tunes. He doesn't want to talk to the priest, but when the latter claims that "all men are equal in God's eyes," Salieri sits up and takes notice. "*Are* they?" he asks with a telling expression on his face. When the priest fails to recognize his old tunes, Salieri begins to play Mozart's "Eine Kleine Nachtmusik," and when he identifies its composer, he places special emphasis on Mozart's middle name, Amadeus, for he is aware of the what the name means, something like "God's beloved."

Though Salieri confesses that he envied as well as admired Mozart even as a child, the ugly side of envy is not going to take a strong hold on him until much later. When Mozart first comes to Vienna, Salieri plays a

102

game whereby he wants to see whether such talent as Mozart has shows. When he eavesdrops on Mozart's scatological jokes as the latter plays a hide-and-seek kind of game with Constanze, his future wife, Salieri is shocked. Not so much by the scatological jokes as by God's having bestowed upon that "giggling, dirty-minded creature" such divine talent. When later he picks up some of Mozart's sheet music, he looks at the notes and hears music he has never heard before, music "filled with longing," with "such unfulfillable longing" that it strikes him as the very "voice of God." And the question immediately arises in his mind: "Why would God choose an obscene child to be His instrument?" (It never occurs to Salieri that perhaps God works in mysterious ways or that, as Mozart himself will put it later, although he is a vulgar man, his music is not.)

When still a young boy Salieri makes a bargain with God (at least a bargain in his own mind): he promises God that if He makes him a famous composer, he shall glorify Him and be kind to others. This resolution is shaken with the advent of Mozart. Although Joseph II will be impressed with Mozart (and rightly so), the committee (as I shall call them), consisting of Salieri as Court Composer, Count Orsini-Rosenberg as the Director of the Opera, Baron Van Swieten as the Imperial Librarian, Kappelmeister Bonno, and Johann Von Strack as the Imperial Chamberlain, will be constantly undermining him in subtle (and at times not so subtle) ways.

Count Orsini-Rosenberg dislikes Mozart from the beginning and thinks of his work as a young man's attempt to impress beyond his means while using "too many notes" in his music (a phrase that will haunt Mozart later on as well). When Mozart first comes to the imperial court, Salieri prepares a little march of welcome for him. The scene that ensues shows a Mozart not wise in the ways of the world, a Mozart who is child-like in his innocence and unaware of the possibility of giving offence. He knows he is talented and he is not shy about this either. At the same time, he is less than diplomatic when he proves not only that he has memorized Salieri's little march upon a single hearing, but also when, while replaying it, he improves upon it with a kind of childish glee. This unintended insult does not escape anyone present, except of course Mozart himself, largely because he had not intended to insult anyone, he was merely taking childish delight in his ability to play and to improve upon the melody he was playing. Salieri is thus not right in taking offense, but he is not wrong either. Such is human nature. We don't like to admit our limitations, and we certainly don't like them exposed in front of others. Mozart's (innocent) thoughtlessness in this regard can probably be attributed to his early experiences as a world-famous prodigy.

With the production of *The Abduction from the Seraglio*, Salieri notices that his pupil, Katherina Cavalieri, has probably had an affair with Mozart. This infuriates him. By this time, though, a certain malice against Mozart has already been at play. The Emperor is pleased with Mozart's opera in German, but he is uncertain about certain parts of it. Count Orsini-Rosenberg takes advantage of the opportunity to chime in with his "too many notes" remark. Mozart's triumph is thereby diminished, to the delight of the "committee." This committee will, in fact, from this point on frequently stand in judgment of Mozart and will actively try to sabotage him as well, whenever possible.

When the scene shifts (as it does from time to time) to the old Salieri and the priest, Salieri once more raises the question: "What was God up to?" At this point he admits that by now he has been "filling up with hatred for" Mozart and that for the first time in his life, he has begun "to know really violent thoughts." When Emperor Joseph II wants to appoint Mozart as tutor for the Princess Elizabeth, Salieri expresses a concern for "favoritism," thus subtly undermining Mozart's chances for this appointment. When a committee is set up to which all applicants need to submit samples of their work (a ploy merely to frustrate Mozart), the trick works well. Mozart's pride intervenes and he refuses to submit samples of his work. When, unbeknownst to him, his wife goes to see Salieri with samples of Mozart's works, original sheets of music in which no corrections have been made, Salieri's envy reaches its apex. As he tells the priest, he was astounded that these were not copies and that there were no corrections of any kind in them. Once more he hears the music he is looking at on the page and once more he asserts that what he hears is "the very voice of God" while "staring through the cage of those meticulous ink-strokes at an absolute beauty."

Old Salieri now admits his utter frustration with God. "If He didn't want me to serve him with music, why implant the desire, like a lust in my body, then deny me the talent?" Back in the story proper, Salieri now declares war on God. He throws a crucifix on the fire in his fireplace and says, in no uncertain terms:

Because you scorn my attempts at virtue; because you choose for your instrument a boastful, lustful, smutty infantile boy and give me for reward only the ability to recognize the Incarnation; because you are unjust, I will block you! I will hinder and harm your creature on earth as far as I am able. I will ruin your Incarnation!

Mozart, of course, has no idea about any of this. When his father arrives from Salzburg, we quickly see that although Mozart is over 25 by now and married and his wife is expecting their first child, Leopold Mozart is still trying to control him. At this point, though, they go out to have some fun and they end up at a Masquerade Ball where they play, among other things, a version of musical chairs. When Mozart has to pay a penalty, he ends up imitating the style of famous composers on a harpsichord. After having imitated the likes of Back and Gluck, he is called upon to do a version of Salieri (by none other than Salieri himself). Mozart does a parody of Salieri that's rather nasty (and he ends the performance with a fart). Once more, as the old Salieri recalls, the person laughing at him wasn't Mozart. As he puts it: "That was not Mozart laughing, Father. That was God. That was God laughing at me through that obscene giggle."

Salieri has by now planted a private spy in Mozart's house, in the person of a maid. Through her agency he finds out that Mozart is working on a new opera, *The Marriage of Figaro*, based on a play banned by the emperor. Once again, the committee gets in the act. They now plot to have the emperor stop the incipient play dead in its tracks. Mozart, however, manages to defend the play and get the emperor's permission to go to rehearsal. Now the committee finds fault with a dance number, which they claim violates the emperor's rule against ballet in his opera. Mozart comes to see Salieri who promises him to talk to the emperor which, of course, he does not. Still, a surprise visit by the emperor gets the music back into the scene, but at the time of the opening performance the emperor happens to yawn, and (naturally) the committee takes this as a joyous sign that the opera (admired, albeit secretly, by Salieri) has but a short run.

When Mozart's father dies, Mozart writes his "blackest opera," *Don Giovanni*. Salieri seems to be the only one who truly understands this opera, in which he sees Mozart trying to deal with the psychological impact of his father-son relation with Leopold Mozart, the controlling father. The play fails in Vienna, but Salieri attends all eight performances it has and secretly worships every single note. At the same time he admits to the priest that the "madness" has now truly begun. He has come up with a scheme (based in part on his interpretation of *Don Giovanni*) that will—or so he thinks—enable him to "kill" Mozart. He acquires the costume Mozart's father had worn at the time they went to a Masquerade Ball (when Mozart had parodied Salieri's music) and comes to commission from Mozart a Requiem Mass. At the same time Schikaneder performs a parody of Mozart's various works in a vaudeville theater in the suburbs of Vienna. The parody is a huge success. When Schikaneder invites Mozart to write a "fantasy" for the "common people," Mozart agrees.

This leads to the eventual production of *The Magic Flute*. But now Mozart is assailed by two incompatible ambitions, to write *The Magic Flute* and to complete the Requiem Mass (both are money-making enterprises but the death mass seems the more likely to pay well). At the same time, Mozart keeps associating the task of writing the Requiem Mass both with his father and with his own perhaps imminent death. In the meantime Constanze leaves him, too. By the time *The Magic Flute* is produced, Mozart is exhausted. He faints before the show is over and is taken home by, of all people, Salieri. Salieri is, of course, hell-bent on finishing the Requiem Mass. His object is to have it performed as his own work at Mozart's funeral. These final scenes are both moving and disturbing. Mozart is clearly exhausted, perhaps near death. So Salieri assists him as they both work on the new composition. What emerges here is very interesting indeed. Salieri sees how a genius goes about composing (in fact, he tells Mozart, quite sincerely, that he is the best composer Salieri knows). What emerges here is just how much Salieri could have learned from Mozart if he had not envied him, if he had not blamed God for the talent God had bestowed upon him.

Things are now quickly coming to a closure. While Constanze is on her way back to Vienna from the spa she had gone to earlier (she has clearly had a change of heart there), Mozart gets way too exhausted to go on with the work and falls asleep. By the time Constanze arrives with Mozart's son Schikaneder will have stopped by with Mozart's take for that night's performance of *The Magic Flute* (which Salieri will let Mozart think came from the mysterious person who has commissioned him to write the Requiem Mass). Upon entering their chambers, Constanze is surprised to find Salieri asleep on the second bed in the room. While the two argue about Salieri's not being welcome there, Mozart wakes up and then dies. He is buried on a rainy day in a common grave. His Requiem Mass in playing in the background.

The denouement takes us back to the old Salieri and the priest. Whether or not Salieri has had an active role in Mozart's untimely death is a moot question. Salieri blames God for it. As he puts it, God "destroyed his beloved rather than let a mediocrity like me get the smallest share in his glory." Salieri's punishment? That while Mozart's music is ever growing in popularity, his (Salieri's) has been completely forgotten in the 30 years since Mozart's dead. As he is pushed in a wheelchair to the water closet and then to have sugar rolls for his breakfast, Salieri blesses all the mediocrities whose patron saint he has declared himself to be.

Though Salieri's motives are clear (and clearly of evil intent), it doesn't really seem possible that he alone has been responsible for Mozart's death. But then it is the intention that counts. Envy alone is among the seven deadly sins. So what's the movie's point? While excellence, such as Mozart's, can be inadvertently offensive, hurt pride, such as Salieri's, can become obsessive and obsessively evil in its intent. Yet excellence survives. Even as Salieri is wheeled away in his wheelchair, we hear Mozart's irritating giggle coming from above, from beyond the grave. Mozart's triumph is the triumph of excellence and immortality. And Salieri's sole consolation is that because he has (he hopes) been inextricably tangled up with Mozart's name as the person who has tried to destroy him, he (along with Mozart's fame) shall enjoy an immortality of sorts, but while Mozart will be famous forever, Salieri will be infamous for the same period of time. A hollow victory, but perhaps the only one available to those who fail to love, to those who try to destroy others, especially when they try to destroy those who are apparently favored by God's undeniable love.

2. The Color Purple

[Movie Log: Released in 1885 by Warner Bros. Screenplay by Menno Meyjes, based on Alice Walker's novel. Directed by Stephen Spielberg. Cast: Whoopi Goldberg (Celie); Danny Glover (Albert); Margaret Avery

Steven C. Scheer

(Shug Avery); Oprah Winfrey (Sofia); Willard E. Pugh (Harpo); Akosua Busia (Nettie); Desreta Jackson (Young Celie); Dana Ivey (Miss Millie)]

> *All this harmonious order of things is achieved by love which rules the earth and the seas, and commands the heavens. / But if love should slack the reigns, all that is now joined in mutual love would wage continual war, and strive to tear apart the world.*
> —Boethius, *The Consolation of Philosophy*

The movie is faithful to the novel to a large extent. There are differences in the stories told, but my purpose here is to treat the movie, so I shall avoid mentioning the discrepancies, treating the movie as if it were the whole story. I do not do this lightly, for I first read the novel (more than once, in fact) and love and admire it immensely. Still this book is about movies, so I shall stick to my resolution here and not worry about what's in the novel (which in many cases is richer and deeper than words can tell, though it is precisely Alice Walker's words that tell it "like it is").

Sisterly love is the commencement of the story, out in the fields resplendent with wild flowers of a purplish hue, Celie and Nettie play a game in which they assert their undying love and loyalty to each other: "Me and you, us never part, makidada, me and you, ain't no ocean, ain't no sea, makidada, keep my sister away from me." In the winter of 1909 Celie, a mere child, gives birth to a baby girl with her sister Nellie acting as the midwife. Her Pa, the father of the baby, immediately takes it away. Celie knows that he will not kill her any more than he has killed a son born to them prior to this. She also knows that her children have been "sold" to a preacher and his wife. The fact that her Pa takes advantage of Celie is the first sign we have in the movie that we are in a world here where men can be brutally selfish. Since Celie's mother (who dies soon) no longer can have sex with her husband, Pa simply takes Celie to be a convenient substitute in total disregard to her own feelings in the matter.

Pa is equally nonchalant when it comes to marrying Celie (who has been "spoiled twice" in his words) off to a widower farmer who has been giving amorous glances to Nettie in church. Albert needs a woman to take care of his house and to tend to his children. Celie isn't his first choice but she will do. Albert, like Celie's Pa, is the epitome of selfishness. And he is not averse to violence either, all in order to show who has the upper hand. When Nettie comes to stay with them, he soon attempts to rape her.

108

Unlike Celie, though, Nettie fights him off (this happens out of view but it's obvious that she has hit him hard in the groin with her satchel full of heavy school books—including a hardbound copy of *Oliver Twist* that she has been using to teach Celie to read).

The vengeful Albert literally throws Nettie off his property, thereby inflicting a cruel and unnatural separation on the loving sisters.

The shaving scene on the porch is the first of two. In this one Celie is timid and fearful of cutting Albert (who threatens to kill her should she do so). The mailman comes and brings news of Shug Avery's intended visit. Celie also gets a letter from Nettie, but she doesn't receive it. It is the first that will be intercepted by Albert, who even tells Celie that he has fixed the mailbox so as to know if she ever "messes" with it. At this point Celie is cut off from her sister as well as from any means of communication between them. She is also cut off from her children. There is a moving scene in the store where the preacher's wife brings Celie's daughter (Olivia) and where Celie can at least for a moment hold her in her arms. She is, of course, not sure that this is her daughter, but something tells her that it is.

Harpo (Celie's stepson) is now in love with a certain Sofia, a feisty young woman full of spirit. She will prove to be a woman who cannot be controlled by her husband. She is carrying Harpo's child prior to their marriage, which Albert opposes on no particular grounds. The marriage does take place, of course, though Harpo's willingness to stand up to his father is perhaps more Sofia's doing than his own. It is nevertheless a contrast between father and son, in that it will emerge that the reason why Albert never married Shug Avery, the love of his life, is because *his* father had opposed the marriage and he wasn't man enough to stand up to him. Harpo would be very happy with Sofia, in spite of the latter's willfulness, but Albert taunts him about not having the upper hand and, when once Harpo asks Celie what he should do about his domineering wife, Celie suggests that he beat her.

Sofia not only fights back (of course), but when she finds out from Harpo at whose suggestion he has acted this way, she comes and lets Celie have it:

All my life I had to fight my daddy, I had to fight my uncle, I had to fight my brothers! Girl child ain't safe in a family of mens, but I never thought I'd fight in my own house! I loves Harpo, God knows I do, but I'll kill him dead before I let him beat me.

Quite a contrast to Celie who, as she says at one point, is not a fighter, only a survivor. Yet the fights, once begun, shall continue between Sofia and Harpo, in spite of the children they will have, until one day Sofia decides to just leave.

In the meantime Albert finally brings Shug Avery to their house. Shug is sick. And Albert aims to please her. He makes a comic figure trying to prepare a meal for her. It is not until Celie takes back their kitchen that Shug begins to eat and to recover. "You sure is ugly" is the first thing she tells Celie upon her arrival. This reinforces Celie's already deeply ingrained lack of self-esteem (her Pa once told her that she had the ugliest smile, which resulted in Celie's frequently holding her hand against her lips in order to hide her smiles). Yet in a relatively short time, the two hit it off. Shug even makes reference to Celie to her father (the local preacher) not knowing that he still loves her. Albert's father doesn't like Shug either. When he comes and disparages her, Celie spits into the glass of water he brings him and says to herself that next time she might even put a "little Shug Avery pee in his glass and see how he like that." It is at this point, too, that Albert admits to loving Shug Avery and expresses a regret for not having married her. He also defends her "honor" by insisting on the fact that all her children (being brought up by Shug's father) are by the same man.

The story now jumps to the year 1922. Harpo and his friend Swain are busy building a "juke joint." It is here that Shug will sing a song called "Miss Celie's Blues," in which she will call her "sister," and encourage her to think of herself as "something, too." Indeed by now the two will be like sisters (watching the movie I have often thought that Shug becomes a kind of surrogate for Nettie), even though there is a touch of lesbianism to their deep and abiding friendship. It is certainly from Shug that Celie will learn that sex is not simply a matter of a man getting on top of a woman and doing his "business" on her (which strikes Shug as if the man went to the toilet on the woman, which is what Celie will say it feels like to her).

When Shug indicates that she is soon going to leave, Celie tells her that Albert beats her, primarily because she (Celie) is not Shug. Shug now goes to see her father, the local preacher, to give him an update about herself, but her father turns his back on her, in spite of Shug's reminding him of a song they used to sing, "God is trying to tell you something," which does no good at all. Now Celie is packing some of her things, as she intends to go with Shug to Memphis. This time, however, the plan will not be carried out. When Albert and Celie accompany Shug to the car that will take her away, Celie falls down in a faint as Shug is driven off.

The movie now picks up Sofia's tragic story. A certain Miss Millie, the mayor's wife, accosts her children. She fancies herself a benefactress of black people, but in reality she is a totally and unscrupulously selfish person. This part of the story is painful to watch, but it does epitomize the deeply dehumanizing streaks that run through racism in its myriads of manifestations. Miss Millie admires (and bestows unwanted kisses on) Sofia's children. She assumes that nothing would make Sofia happier than to come and work for her as her maid. When Sofia responds to this uncalled-for suggestion with a "Hell, no!" her fate is sealed. When the mayor slaps her (we know what Sofia does to those who slap her) even Swain, Harpo's friend, who is nearby, is horror-stricken at what it about to happen. Sofia makes a fist and knocks the mayor down. Pandemonium ensues and Sofia ends up in jail. She is severely beaten, too.

The twenty-year sentence she receives is way out of proportion for her "crime." Yet she is now, for all intents and purposes, in the situation of a "slave." Arrangements are made for her to be released from prison on condition that she accepts the position as Miss Millie's maid, after all. One of the most chilling scenes in the movie involves Miss Millie's alleged "benevolence." Sofia is teaching her how to drive. She finally allows Sofia to go home and see her children. It is Christmas and Sofia hasn't seen her children in eight years. Miss Millie drives her out into the country where the whole "clan" is awaiting her with tender loving care. But Miss Millie has trouble getting the car to behave and then mistakes the intentions of the men who try to assist her. She becomes hysterical (claims that they were trying to "attack" her) and won't let anyone drive her home in order to let Sofia spend more time with her children. The look on Miss Millie's face is a horror to behold. It says something like: how dare you think of spending more time with your children when I "need" you to take me home! Every time I ˌsee the movie, I think of Miss Millie's facial expression in this scene as the face of evil in that it is in utter disregard of the humanity of another.

The story now jumps from the 1930 (where the previous scene took place) to 1936. There is joy in Albert's house as Shug Avery is coming back, but when she comes with a husband in tow, both Albert and Celie are a bit taken aback. The two men get drunk and talk in friendly acknowledgement of each other's roles in Shug's life, while Shug checks the mailbox (she is expecting something from Memphis) and finds Nettie's latest letter to Celie. This leads to the discovery that Albert, in an act of senseless vengeance and cruelty, has been hiding Nettie's letters from Celie for many, many years. The two women search for and find the letters and there is great joy in learning that Nettie is a missionary in Africa where she has gone with the preacher and his wife who have "adopted" Celie's children.

All is not "fun and games" in Africa either. The inhabitants of the village of Olinka are set in their ways. They don't believe that girls should be educated (thus they are compared to white people in America, who don't want black people to learn). And we also find out that white people in Africa are as totally indifferent to the humanity and the needs of the natives as racists tend to be anywhere on the face of this earth. The road builders, for example, totally disregard the village of Olinka and raze whatever buildings (including the church and school built by the missionaries) happen to be in the way of their plans. Yet there is good news in Nettie's letters, too. For one thing, they are planning to come back to America, provided they can work out certain problems with Immigration about their nationality.

Something in Celie has now snapped, though. Knowing Albert's perfidy does not sit well with her. And as she is about to shave him, we feel that she might just cut his throat this time. Shug seems to intuit this, too, so she comes running back to the house. In the meantime scenes are effectively intercut between Celie and the razor in her hand and a face-slicing ritual in Africa. In fact, a number of scenes are intercut between the two continents, thus establishing a kind of "vision" for Celie, which represents the power of the written word that Nettie's letters bring in their wake. Shug arrives just in time to, literally, save Albert's neck.

In the dinner scene that ensues a new Celie emerges. Shug informs the whole family that Celie is going with them to Memphis. Celie now calls Albert "a low-down, dirty dog." It is the first time in all these years that she has spoken negative words to him. She tells him in no uncertain terms that he has separated her from Nettie, the only person in the world who truly loved her, and she informs him that Nettie is coming back to America, bringing Celie's children with her, and that, collectively, they'll "whoop" his "ass." She also tells Harpo that if he "hadn't tried to rule over Sofia, white folks wouldn't have got her." When she calls Albert "horseshit," Sofia starts to laugh. All the women start to laugh. Even Harpo's suggestion that it is "bad luck for women to laugh at a man" is unable to stop them.

Something happens here, and the indictment of male domination is the least of it. Sofia now makes a very moving speech in which we get a glimpse into the goodness that has been animating Celie all along. This also provides us with a glimpse into the power of love to rejuvenate, to wipe out the evils of the past, to move towards reconciliation unheard of without this power. Sofia says:

> I wanna thank you, Miss Celie, for everything you done for me. I remember that day I was in the store with Miss Millie. I was feelin' real down. I was feelin' mighty bad, and when I see'd you, I knowed there is a God, and one day I was gonna get to come home.

The ties of love bind in unaccountable ways. A mere glimpse, a kind word, can move mountains. Though Celie's anger is understandable, it is to her credit that she puts the knife down she holds against Albert's throat when he has the effrontery to suggest that he won't give her any money. Celie now "curses" Albert and tells him that "until [he] does right by [her]," everything he touches or thinks of shall fail and that he is going to rot in the "jail" he has planned for her.

By the fall of 1937 Albert admits to his Pa that his life is "already ruined. This house is dead. There ain't no Shug, ain't no chil'un, ain't no laughter, ain't no life." There is only "just" him. Things happen in rapid succession now. Celie utilizes her talent to sew to start a business of her own. Meanwhile her Pa dies ("on top" of his new, young wife), and the truth comes out. He wasn't Celie's biological father, who was lynched, actually, and through whom, by means of her mother, Celie and Nettie inherit the house and store her Pa inhabited all these years.

It is here, out in the fields one day, amidst myriads of wild flowers, that Celie and Shug discuss God and His love and how He encourages us to admire His creation and all the good things in it. This is a very curtailed version of the section of the novel (I know I said I wouldn't bring the novel up) I have always nicknamed the "theology chapter." Nevertheless, like in the novel, it is here that the title of both the novel and the movie jumps out at us. It comes up in Shug's splendid remark that "it pisses God off if you walk by the color purple in a field somewhere and don't notice it." This "theology" scene is followed by a convergence between Shug Avery and the "juke joint" folk (a whole crowd of musicians and patrons) and the church service that's being conducted at the same time by Shug's father, the local preacher. The preacher's text is "prodigal children," whom the Lord can bring home. The old song, "God is trying to tell you something," is now sung both by the choir in the church and Shug Avery leading the crowd on the road that takes us to the church. The church choir and Shug Avery are now singing in unison ("God is trying to tell you something"), and as she enters the church, at the head of the "juke joint" procession, her father looks straight at her and his stern visage is softened into a smile. Father and daughter embrace and, at long last, a heart-warming reconciliation takes place.

In the meantime Albert finds a letter in his mailbox from the Immigration and Naturalization Service. We see him take the letter to the appropriate office. He is now obviously intervening on Celie's (and Nettie's) behalf, though he does this behind the scenes, where he will now remain to the end. This kind act on his part leads to Nettie's return from Africa with Celie's children, who are now grown. Adam, her son, is married to an African woman and Olivia, her daughter, is an accomplished and beautiful young woman. Albert is watching this joyous reunion from a distance. In the final scenes of the movie we see Celie and Nettie again as when they were children, clapping each other's hands in playful harmony as their little song asserts (this time for sure) that nothing can separate them. As the final credits roll we hear, once again Shug's Song of Celie's Blues: "Oh sister, you've been on my mind, Oh sister, we are two of a kind. Oh sister have I got news for you. I'm something, I hope you think you are something, too."

The power of love has accomplished miracles. This time it's not romantic love, but the familial and filial love that has been emerging all along against incredible odds. Particularly the love that women are capable of. And what we witness here is not simply the kind of love associated with one's duty, but the love that springs from the hearts of those who are kind or who are capable of achieving kindness. This is the redemptive love that only the best of religiosity can implant in our hearts. Not the stern orthodoxy, the judgmental strictures of the letter, but the fluid, the amorphous beating of hearts fired by something deeper than duty, fired by something so profoundly human that it will even endure the most terrifying hours of the darkest nights of the soul and still remain intact.

3. Malcolm X

[Movie Log: Released in 1992 by Warner Bros. Screenplay by Arnold Perl and Spike Lee, based on *The Autobiography of Malcolm X*, as told to Alex Haley. Directed by Spike Lee. Cast: Denzel Washington (Malcolm X); Angela Bassett (Betty Shabazz); Kate Vernon (Sophia); Delroy Lindo (West Indian Archie); Spike Lee (Shorty); Albert Hall (Baines); Al Freeman, Jr. (Elijah Muhammad); Jean LaMarre (Benjamin 2X)]

> *I don't care what points I made in the interviews, it practically never got printed the way I said it. I was learning under fire how the press, when it wants to, can twist, and slant. If I had said "Mary had a little lamb," what probably would have appeared was "Malcolm X lampoons Mary."*
> —*The Autobiography of Malcolm X*

When I first saw this movie, at the time of its original release, I knew only the "basics" about Malcolm X: that he was a famous black leader—rather militant—and that he was assassinated in the mid 1960s. I walked out of that theater a different person. I was both deeply moved and saddened by what I had just seen. And the next day I picked up my old copy of *The Autobiography of Malcolm X* (purchased many years prior to this, but collecting dust all the while) and read it, for the first time, almost in one fell swoop. I couldn't put it down, not because I wanted to see what "happened next," but because I heard a voice in it so authentic and true that I felt compelled to listen, as if under a spell, until the final words in it "spoken" by Malcolm X (by then El-Hajj Malik El-Shabazz), spoken with the characteristic humility of a saint or holy man: "all of the credit is due to Allah. Only the mistakes have been mine."

To compress an entire life (even a short one) into three and a half hours is no easy feat. Add to that the desire to be truthful (inasmuch as humanly possible) as well as to correct innumerable misconceptions, and the task may well appear to be downright impossible. Yet Spike Lee has managed to do it. Art, of course, need not present the truth literally. It can explore and expose it in characteristic structures. Spike Lee didn't alter the truth of Malcolm X's story even when he changed certain facts (though such changes are few and far between—and anyone who knows both the book and the movie well can tell what they are). The changes were undoubtedly made for the sake of dramatic effect (or unity), which need not undermine the truth of a story. For buried in the story of Malcolm X, the man, the human person, is a universal "structure" or archetype that history has seen before. The specifics of Malcolm X's life carry with them a burden that has more than one face. First, the story is about oppression and the brave and uncompromising call to throw off the oppression in question. Second, it is also the story of misunderstandings, misinterpretations, and misconceptions; how and why they come into play (and how we may learn to avoid them).

Some have questioned Spike Lee's opening with footage of the members of the Los Angeles Police Department beating Rodney King (a familiar sight to most Americans in the days of the movie's release). It seems to me that the opening is an appropriate reminder of what is still and ever possible in a society that has never quite been able to divest itself of racism, overt or covert. The image of the American flag burning until only a large X in the middle of the screen remains is perhaps another symbol of the "unknown" (the still uncertain present and the future), the "unknown" that also signifies Malcolm Little's lost name. But there is more to this life story than the defiance of oppression and the consequent maze of misunderstandings, misinterpretations, and misconceptions that the defiance in question brings in its wake. As we see the Rodney King footage interspersed with the image of the burning flag, we first hear a voice asking, "Who do we want to hear?" followed by the rousing response, "Malcolm X." Then we hear the man himself as he charges the white man with crimes against the black man, as he tells his black brothers and sisters that they are not Americans, but the "victims of America," and as he asserts that, as black people, they "have never seen democracy," they "have only seen hypocrisy." All this goes by fast, as the credits roll, but already we must pause and reflect on what we have seen and heard to this point: an appeal to hear what Malcolm X is really saying. From this point of view the Rodney King footage is appropriate, as is the image of the burning flag. From a strictly black point of view America is indeed a hypocrisy rather than a democracy and the black man has indeed been its victim. From a broad and uncompromising perspective, this is indeed undeniable, which any honest person devoid of prejudices or illusions must admit. For indeed, in large part, the most significant theme of *Malcolm X* is the discrepancy between what is and what people say is, between what Malcolm X is saying and what (white) people think he is saying.

The story itself picks up in Boston during the war years. Shorty straightens Malcolm's hair. Since it's reddish in color, Malcolm's nickname at this point is Red (or Detroit Red). As the two walk towards the dance hall in their "zoot suits," we get our first flashback to the KKK coming to the Little house at the time Malcolm's mother was pregnant with him. They break the windows of the Little house and ride off in the light of a vastly enlarged moon. The flashback moves on to Malcolm's father, a Baptist minister preaching a "back to Africa" message to his congregation. This urging the blacks to separate from the whites and to be their own masters will, of course, also be the message of the Black Muslims so eloquently "preached" by Malcolm X himself later on. The scene now switches to the dance hall where Detroit Red meets Sophia, the white woman who will become his lover until their arrest. At this point Malcolm chooses the white woman over the black Laura (partly out of a sense of nobility—he doesn't want to "ruin" the latter, a church-going young woman—although she will later become a prostitute). The day after, in the park, Shorty and Malcolm engage in a mock gunfight in which Malcolm is shot (the first of several such foreshadowings).

The flashbacks in the first phase of Malcolm's life (the phase during which he is Detroit Red, a numbers runner, a pimp, a drug user, and a burglar) quickly reveal to us that his childhood is the archetypal black experience: encounters with the KKK, the lynching (for all intents and purposes) of his father (where white Christian is against black Christian—one reason for Malcolm's later rejection of Christianity in favor of Islam), the state's disruption of the family, the children being parceled out into various foster homes, the mother ending up in a state institution thanks to a more or less permanent nervous breakdown she suffers as a result of all this. And why? Simply because Malcolm's father was preaching a "doctrine" disapproved of by certain white people. Add to this Malcolm's being told by a teacher that the likes of him cannot aspire to the law, that at best he could only be a carpenter (it is perhaps ironic that the teacher should mention that Jesus was a carpenter, too) and we shouldn't be surprised by Malcolm's turning his back on school and, eventually, on the workaday world in general.

His job on a train brings Malcolm to New York, to Harlem, where he quickly meets West Indian Archie (it is at this point that he begins his life of crime as a numbers runner). This relationship deteriorates when Archie, who never writes anything down, challenges Malcolm's claim to certain winning numbers. Since West Indian Archie's "reputation is on the line," Malcolm is forced to flee to Boston with Sophia and Shorty. The flashback here is rather telling. We see the Little house set on fire by a white supremacist group and we get the second image of Malcolm's father's death on the streetcar tracks. The criminal world is no kinder to the likes of Malcolm than the world of the white supremacists. Which is partly the reason why Malcolm will find it so easy to convert to Islam, when the opportunity comes. Which is just around the corner. Their life as burglars in Boston quickly comes to an end, and while Sophia and Shorty's girlfriend (both white) get two years each, Malcolm and Shorty get 14 counts of 8 to 10 years each, primarily because their crime wasn't just burglary but also sleeping with white women.

Malcolm is at first defiant in prison. Having been a numbers runner, he is now a number. And when he refuses to recite his prison number, he is thrown into solitary confinement until his spirit is apparently (though only apparently) broken. It is in the shower that Baines, a fellow prisoner and a Black Muslim, first approaches Malcolm. The second phase of his life, the phase during which he comes to be known as Malcolm X, now commences. Baines tells Malcolm that a certain Elijah Muhammad can get him out of prison. He doesn't mean the physical prison, of course, but the prison of the mind. Baines encourages Malcolm to "read and study," and to "quit taking the white man's poison—his cigarettes, liquor, women, and pork." The beginning of Malcolm X's education is telling. Baines guides him to the dictionary definitions of "black" and "white," where the first is surrounded by highly negative, while the second is surrounded by highly positive connotations. Baines urges Malcolm to "go behind the words and find out the truth." He also tells him that if he takes "one step toward Allah, Allah will take two steps toward" him.

The Black Muslim view of the white man is just as one-sided as the white man's view is of the black man, but it is an understandable counterview, a reasonable reaction. In any case, Malcolm X quickly embraces the idea that God is black, that the white man is the devil, that blacks are of the Tribe of Shabazz "lost in the wilderness of America." Baines also explains to Malcolm that Islam means "submission," though Malcolm will at first find it next to impossible to go down on his knees and ask God's (Allah's) forgiveness. Not until after he gets a letter from the Honorable Elijah Muhammad will he be able to kneel. And soon he will dedicate his "life to telling the white devil the truth to his face." It will be this aspect of Malcolm X's "message" that will be at the center or heart of his mission as a Black Muslim, and it will be the white man's denial of what is broadly and generally true in this "message" that will be behind all the misunderstandings and misinterpretations and misrepresentations of Malcolm X by all those who choose not to hear what he is really saying. Whenever Malcolm X will talk of the black man's right to defend himself, for example, the white man will always hear something else: a call to arms by all blacks against all whites. His message of self-defense will always be construed as a message of hate, in spite of repeated assertions that what the Honorable Elijah Muhammad teaches blacks is not to hate whites, but to love themselves.

When Malcolm X is released from prison and finally meets the Honorable Elijah Muhammad in person, he is a changed man. Having educated himself in prison (by, among other things, the legendary copying out of the entire dictionary), Malcolm quickly becomes a minister. From the very beginning he is extremely articulate and charismatic. The Muslim message is clear: blacks need to take charge of themselves on all fronts, including the economic. They need to get out of the prison of the mind, and they must not succumb to the turn-the-other-cheek philosophy, because "white Christians hang black Christians from trees." The Muslim view is non-compromising on seeing the white man as the devil. Not that some white men are devils, mind you, but that the entire race is evil. There is, of course, some truth to the sense of hypocrisy ineluctably built into white culture, which is clearly present in the discrepancy between the Declaration of Independence asserting that "all men are created equal" and the unequivocal denial of this by the institution of slavery and by the subsequent continuation of segregation even when the latter is, according to decree, clearly against the law.

Malcolm X is now truly a changed man. Not only does he "preach" the doctrine of the Honorable Elijah Muhammad, but he also keeps himself to the strict demands of Muslim morality (something he is not going to deviate from till the end of his life). His courtship of Betty Shabazz (née Betty Saunders) is utterly charming. Their potential union is obviously approved of by, among others, Baines, but their feeling for each other is nonetheless absolutely genuine. The Honorable Elijah Muhammad's take on women is somewhat ambivalent. He doesn't trust the "fair sex," at the same time he favors marriage between the right partners. Malcolm X follows suit. He asks for Betty's hand in marriage over the phone, between engagements, and the union is quickly finalized by a Muslim ceremony. For the remainder of their marriage (and the remainder of Malcolm X's life), Betty will be a strong force in the minister's mission. Their love and loyalty will be tested, but never threatened, no matter what.

The first sign of Malcolm X's rising power as a minister is given during the time a certain Brother Johnson is attacked and wounded by the police. The great crowd that follows Malcolm first to the police station and then to the hospital is aided and abetted by a large number of non-Muslims also coming up in the wake of the procession. When the police captain who comes to try to disperse the crowd sees the control Malcolm X wields over this highly disciplined crowd, he will exclaim "that's too much power for one man to have." This is yet another foreshadowing, this time a foreshadowing of the betrayal that awaits Malcolm. By now he is the Honorable Elijah Muhammad's "national minister" and clearly the major spokesperson of the Nation of Islam. As such he is more and more in the news and more and more misinterpreted and misunderstood, even by other black leaders. He remains, of course, non-compromising and steadfast in his message.

During a television appearance, for example, he is challenged by both whites and blacks. It is here that we get the famous distinction between the "house Negro" and the "field Negro," an allegory about those who—for the sake of a subservient existence—are willing to abide with the white man as opposed to those who want to separate and run away from the cruel master. Ironically it is not the white man who will start to turn against Malcolm X. It will be Baines, the man who originally "saved" him in prison, who will start to whisper in the Honorable Elijah Muhammad's ears that the "brothers think that Malcolm is getting too much press." At this point the Honorable Elijah Muhammad defends Malcolm, but perhaps the seed is planted. In the immediate aftermath Malcolm X's success as a black minister grows. He now gives lectures at places like Harvard where he clearly indicates that what the Honorable Elijah Muhammad has accomplished is something the white community should be grateful for: he has turned innumerable black criminals away from a life of crime.

Given the present situation, as the Black Muslims see it, the only solution to America's racial problems is "the complete separation between the black race and the white race." Ironically, this is reminiscent of the segregation practiced in the South, but with a decisive difference. What the Black Muslims want is to have control over their own lives on every front, including the economic. At this point, in a sense, the position of the Black Muslims is the other side of the proverbial coin. It is the mirror image of the white position as the Black Muslims see it. At the heart of the conflict is the Black Muslim view according to which, under the white man's present practices (as opposed to possible liberal theories), no real integration is possible.

By this time Malcolm X is aware of "talk" among the brothers, talk which implicates a certain jealousy concerning his high visibility and obvious popularity among the masses of Black Muslims. He is nevertheless unshakably loyal to the Honorable Elijah Muhammad. When Betty broaches another subject, that of the Honorable Elijah Muhammad's various paternity cases, Malcolm's first reaction is to see this as nothing but slander, the white man's attempt to destroy the reputation of a truly holy man. It is Betty who tells him that although he is ready to face death on a daily basis, the possibility of betrayal never occurs to him. Malcolm X goes to see several women who have had children by the Honorable Elijah Muhammad. From them he also learns that the Honorable Elijah Muhammad thinks of him as his greatest minister, but also as one who is going to leave him. Thus the possibility of betrayal rears its ugly head. Malcolm now goes to see Baines who excuses the Honorable Elijah Muhammad on the grounds that he is human and that the likes of Noah, David, and Solomon were not perfect either yet they did the work of God. Malcolm both accepts and rejects this view. As he tells us, his faith has now been "shattered."

When the assassination of John Fitzgerald Kennedy doesn't soften Malcolm X's view of the white man and he makes statements that seem highly unfeeling and insensitive (the famous—or infamous—remarks about the chickens coming home to roost), the Honorable Elijah Muhammad takes advantage of this "blunder" and silences Malcolm X for 90 days. As a true Muslim, Malcolm submits 100 percent (a reminder that Islam means submission, too, of course). But now things change.

Threatening phone calls are beginning to be made. One of Malcolm's loyal followers admits that he has been given a "mission" to wire Malcolm's car. With characteristic nobility and unselfishness Malcolm dismisses this loyal follower in order to assure his (the follower's) safety.

The year is now 1964. Malcolm calls a press conference during which he announces his separation from the Honorable Elijah Muhammad. From this point on, he says, he is going to be his own man. He intends to open the lines of communication between himself and others, those black leaders he had heretofore shunned, as well as whites (who can help but not join the Muslims, since before the blacks can truly cooperate with whites they must first learn to unite among themselves). The new organization will be called Muslim Mosque, Inc. As a result of this new development Malcolm X decides to make his pilgrimage to Mecca (something that's required of every Muslim at least once in a lifetime). The pilgrimage will lead to a final conversion and the last (and—alas—shortest phase) of Malcolm X's life.

What Malcolm X will discover in Mecca is an earth-shattering realization that a point of view other than the one he has been non-compromisingly holding onto up to now is possible, a point of view that sees all of humanity as belonging to the same human family, where the unity of Islamic brotherhood transcends ethnic and racial differences in practice as well as in theory (something that Christianity has not been able to achieve in practice at least). His thinking undergoes a radical shift here from the general to the individual. While the white man in general may be guilty of all that the black man in general can accuse him of, white individuals in particular may be innocent of the crimes committed in times past (or even in the present) against the blacks. We all belong to certain groups, but we don't all share all the characteristics of a certain group. The realization that given individuals may not, in fact, be guilty of the white man's crimes is a horrendous one. Things are (if you will) no longer black and white. Things are now all shades of the rainbow.

Upon his return to America Malcolm X (though now he will call himself El-Hajj Malik El Shabazz) is ready to continue the fight for human (rather than just for civil) rights, but now his enemies (probably mostly from the ranks of the Nation of Islam, though Spike Lee opens the possibility that the Muslims may not be acting alone) are not willing to let bygones be bygones. The threatening phone calls continue. His house is firebombed (Spike Lee once again resorts to flashbacks to the time the

Little house was burned by white supremacists). Malcolm sees this for what it is, an attempt on his life, though Baines (with what seems to me an evil grin) will claim that this is just a "publicity stunt" perpetrated by Malcolm X himself. What follows is painful to watch. The threats and threatening phone calls continue. Malcolm X checks into a hotel to prepare for his new mission, a new address he intends to deliver in the Audubon Ballroom in Harlem. In the meantime his wife and children are staying elsewhere, under the protection of Malcolm's loyal followers.

We now see the assassins sitting around a table getting their guns, the murder weapons, ready. This is an ominous sight. In the meantime representatives of the authorities (the FBI, the CIA?) are eavesdropping on Malcolm's phone conversation with Betty. The next day we see various cars drive towards the Audubon Ballroom. One contains Betty and the children; another, the assassins. And yet another Malcolm X himself. Upon arrival, one of the assassins picks up one of Malcolm's daughter's black dolls. This, too, is an ominous scene. But it is just part and parcel of the inevitable end, the end that has already become history years before the making of the movie. Still, the movie brings it all home in a fresh new way, so that the viewer's pain in quite genuine. Before Malcolm X comes to the podium to speak, he is both restless and saddened. The words of Benjamin 2X's introduction are a compelling reminder of the "theme" of misunderstandings, misinterpretations, and misrepresentations. He says: "And I pray that you and I will listen! Listen, hear, and understand." Which is precisely what the assassins will not do. They will proceed with their foreordained mission with merciless exactitude and shatter, perhaps forever, our own faith in a humanity capable of transcending its own bent on misunderstandings, misinterpretations, and misrepresentations.

Ossie Davis's famous eulogy delivered in the Faith Temple Church of God in Harlem on February 27, 1965 will also invoke this "theme." To those who may still call Malcolm X a "fanatic" and a "racist," this is what Ossie Davis has to say:

> Did you ever talk to Brother Malcolm? Did you ever touch him, or have him smile at you? Did you ever really listen to him? Did he ever do a mean thing? Was he ever himself associated with violence or any public disturbance? For it you did you would know him. And if you knew him you would know why we must honor him: Malcolm was our manhood, our living, black manhood! This

was his meaning to his people. And, in honoring him, we honor the best in ourselves.

It's clear that many never really listened to him. Spike Lee's movie should make us listen though, at long last, and hear and understand. The real story (Malcolm X's life) may have ended tragically, but the story that transcends it is, once again in the words of Ossie Davis, "unconquered still." Which is why school children everywhere can rightly repeat endlessly "I am Malcolm X," and which is why, in the movie, we end with Nelson Mandela's repetition of Malcolm X's own words: "We declare our right on this earth to be a man, to be a human being, to be respected as a human being, in this society, on this earth, in this day, which we intend to bring into existence by any means necessary."

4. Fargo

[Movie Log: Released in 1996 by Polygram Filmed Entertainment in association with Working Title Films. Screenplay by Joel Coen and Ethan Coen. Director: Joel Coen. Cast: William H. Macy (Jerry Lundegaard); Steve Buscemi (Carl Showalter); Peter Stormare (Gaear Grimsrud); Frances McDormand (Marge Gunderson); Kristin Rudrüd (Jean Lundegaard); Harve Presnell (Wade Gustavson)]

> *The love of money is the root of all evil.*
> —1 Timothy, 6:10

Although usually quoted as "money is the root of all evil," it is not money per say that the biblical statement is against, but avarice, covetousness, or cupidity—in short, greed. The quote is also familiar to many in its Latin version as *radix malorum est cupiditas*, which is the way the passage occurs in the Vulgate version of the Bible (and which is also the version used by Chaucer, for example, in *The Canterbury Tales*). *Fargo* is a movie that clearly illustrates this truth, as well as the fact that once an evil plot is unleashed there is no telling where it may end up. Jerry Lundegaard, a hapless car salesman with money problems considered a "loser" by Wade Gustavson, his well-to-do father-in-law and the owner of the car dealership for which Jerry works, comes up with a simple "plot"

124

(as he sees it) which would force his father-in-law to fork over a large sum of money to him indirectly. Through a worker (an ex-con) in the garage of the dealership in which he works Jerry arranges to meet with two unsavory characters who are to kidnap his wife. He gives them a brand new car from his father-in-law's dealership and tells them that they are to split the $80,000 ransom money (they get the new car to begin with and the $40,000 when the "deal" is brought to fruition). Right from the beginning, though, Jerry entangles himself in lies as well as illegalities. This combined with the inaptitude of all parties involved in this supposedly simple plot will be responsible for the senseless and tragic loss of innocent lives the plot unleashes.

Fargo is based on a true story that took place in Minnesota in 1987. The title is taken from the name of the town in North Dakota bordering Minnesota though much of the action takes place in Brainerd and Minneapolis. It is in Fargo that Jerry hands over the keys to the tan Ciera, and it is here that we find out the ill-fated plot he has concocted. Even Carl Showalter, the talkative would-be kidnapper, questions the wisdom of the plot (it strikes him as robbing Peter to pay Paul). The fact that Jerry thinks of this whole scheme as both an "innocent" (no one is supposed to get hurt) and workable enterprise leads us to question his judgment. It will soon become apparent, though, that he is not leveling with his hirelings. He will tell his father-in-law that the ransom is one million dollars. It seems that he is a lot greedier than meets the eye. And Wade Gustavson, the father-in-law, isn't a very likable character either. He certainly has his share of greed. Jean, Jerry's wife, and Scotty, his son, are wonderful, of course, which makes Jerry's plot against his wife—and indirectly against his son as well—("innocently" as he thinks the whole "deal" will transpire) just that much more callous and deplorable. He seems to have no feeling for the undue suffering even a "pretend" kidnapping is likely to inflict upon his wife. To trust the likes of Carl Showalter and Graear Grimsrud, even if the latter comes recommended by a mechanic at the Gustavson dealership, the ex-con Shep Proudfoot, is based on what will soon prove to be an ill-conceived assumption.

Once he returns from Fargo to the suburbs of Minneapolis, the plot has been sat in motion. When it appears that Wade might give him money for a deal he is working on concerning a future parking lot, Jerry goes to see Shep to try to stop the kidnapping, but Shep has no way of getting in touch with the would-be kidnappers. Jerry is also in a bind with respect to the serial number of the car he has handed over to the grim twosome. So things are already not quite working according to plan. But when Wade and his accountant prove unaccommodating with respect to the "deal" for which Jerry is seeking financing, he feels that the plot of kidnapping is his only chance, after all, to get money out of the apparently rather ungenerous Wade. When he returns home with two bags of groceries, he finds his house in a shambles. Jean has already been kidnapped.

Soon the evil planted by this "innocent" plot will explode. When a state trooper stops the grim twosome because the tan Ciera has no temporary license plate displayed, and when the foolish Carl thinks he can bribe the police officer, and when the burlap-bagged Jean in the back seat starts to whimper, Gaear grabs the police officer by the hair, bangs his head against the car door, grabs a gun from the glove compartment, and shoots the state trooper in the head. When a car comes by with potential witnesses, Gaear drives after it and shoots both its occupants in cold blood. Thus the whole "deal" (a word frequently used by Jerry) has already gotten out of control. Because of a careless mistake (not displaying the temporary license plate on the car—shouldn't Jerry have placed the tag there to begin with?), three people are dead on the highway near Brainerd (where previously Carl and Gaear had spent a night in a motel in the company of two prostitutes).

It is at this point that the true "hero" of the story (perhaps one of the most admirable characters in all literature) enters the picture. This is the pregnant Marge Gunderson, Brainerd's chief of police. Our first acquaintance with her and her husband, Norm, immediately establishes a telling contrast between the greed (and its accompanying inaptitude) we have seen so far and the gentle and enviable love that can exist between a man and woman, a husband and a wife. A phone call in the pre-dawn hours awakens Marge about the triple homicide we have just witnessed. Once on the scene, she will quickly prove to be quite an interpreter, quite a sleuth, and quite a detective. She quickly figures out what has transpired. This unassuming but brilliant and amazingly competent and patient policewoman will eventually unravel the whole plot, but how the plot itself unfolds, how the story is structured, is itself of some interest in this chronicle of an evil gone berserk.

When Jerry "discovers" his wife's kidnapping he practices (rehearses) the way in which he is going to pass the news on to his father-in-law. He wants to sound sincere. For the moment Jerry will seem to be holding all the cards. Although Wade considers informing the authorities, Jerry (with the help of Wade's accountant) convinces him that he (Jerry) should be able to handle the "deal." Jerry is, after all, the one who stands to pocket nearly the entire million-dollar ransom. In the meantime Marge gets a lead on the grim twosome. The authorities know what kind of car the state trouper stopped (a tan Ciera), so when Marge is informed that the night before the killings two men checked into a nearby hotel (where they had company), Marge has a chance to talk to the two prostitutes. The scene is suffused with a kind of gentle humor, a thing that runs through the entire movie, thus providing us with another contrast between the "evil that men do" and the possibility of a loving and jovial existence on the other side, as it were, of the horror.

In the meantime the kidnappers settle into a lakeside cabin out in the countryside where they keep Jean, Jerry's kidnapped wife, hooded and tied to a chair. Jean is a feisty woman but from the moment she is kidnapped (with the shower curtain over her head) she remains hooded until her death. I will not attribute any symbolism to this, as it is a believable and realistic detail (the kidnappers don't want her to be ever able to identify them), but if we can't help feeling that there is something telling about her not being able to see what is going on around her, that she is kept from seeing the utter evil unleashed by her greedy husband, so be it. Carl and Gaear certainly treat her with the utmost indifference, a thing that Jerry is guilty of as well—he pays absolutely no attention to how the actual kidnapping might transpire. He simply assumes that his accomplices will do the right thing by her (and certainly expects them not to hurt her).

In the abrupt cut from the lakeside cabin where Carl is attempting to get the TV to behave (the reception is bad) to Marge's home (where she and her husband are watching the TV in bed) there is another telling contrast between the story we are watching and the program in progress on television. We see an insect carry a worm and we hear the TV voice-over say: "The bark beetle carries the worm to the nest, where it will feed its young for up to six weeks." In other words, even insects take better care of their own kind than *some* human beings. Of course, the pregnant Marge (seven months pregnant to boot) and her ever-loving husband, Norm, represent an ongoing contrast between greed (and its unexpected consequences) and a quietly unassuming and contented and loving life that's also possible on this earth.

In the meantime Jerry gets a call from Carl and finds out about the triple homicide near Brainerd. He is by now quite aware that things are not going according to plan. At the same time Marge gets information that is quietly leading her closer and closer to Jerry. She learns of several phone calls made by the two men who checked into that motel near Brainerd and thus obtains Shep Proudfoot's phone number and comes to question him at the Gustavson dealership. She also talks to Jerry, wanting to know if the dealership misses a tan Ciera. At this point Jerry is apparently unperturbed by this "close call," as it were, but we can see the relentless pursuit that's quietly in progress in the rather capable hands of Marge Gunderson, Brainerd's chief of police. There are several episodes that may seem oddly misplaced in the story. The first of these is Marge's meeting with a former classmate, Mike Yanagita, who suddenly phones her late one evening (and calls her Margie Olmstead, her maiden name). When in Minneapolis Marge actually meets with Mike in the restaurant of the hotel where she is staying, we see a somewhat unstable character come on to her and we see the kindness with which she rebuffs him. Later she will learn that the story Mike told about another former schoolmate of theirs (whom he supposedly married and who died of leukemia) is not really true at all, that Mike has been beset by psychological problems. The other episode that seems to have no rhyme or reason in the story involves an escort that Carl picks up and takes to a room somewhere where they are engaged in sex when the outraged Shep Proudfoot busts in on them and violently beats Carl with his belt. Again, the viewer (perhaps at first puzzled by these episodes seemingly unrelated to the story at hand) may find in them yet another telling contrast in the movie chock full of contrasts between the consequences of greed and those of love.

When Wade insists on taking the million-dollar ransom to the appointed place on the top of the Radisson parking lot himself, Jerry's plot gets completely undone, the money will—it seems—never be his. When Carl shoots Wade (and Wade shoots Carl in the face, though this wound is not fatal) things are really totally out of control. When Jerry arrives at the scene he finds his father-in-law dead, the million dollars gone, and even the attendant in the Exit Booth shot to death. In the meantime Carl stops the car on the highway somewhere and looks in the briefcase. He removes $80,000 from it and buries the case with the rest of the money in the snow next to a fence on the highway. He sticks an ice scraper into the snow there so as to be able to find the money later. Just as Jerry was planning to pocket the rest of the ransom money, Carl is now attempting to do the same. By the time he gets back to the lakeside cabin, bloody face and all, Jean appears to be dead. As Gaear explains, she started to scream. Carl hands Gaear's share of the money over to him. But when he insists on keeping the tan Ciera himself, Gaear follows him outside and kills him with an axe.

In the meantime, still in search of the tan Ciera, Marge comes to see Jerry at the dealership again. He behaves rather erratically and, eventually, "flees the interview." Later, driving near Moose Lake, Marge will hear on her police phone about how Jerry Lundegaard claims his wife was kidnapped on the day of the triple homicide near Brainerd. By this time she will also learn that Jerry's father-in-law is missing as well. Just as this is transpiring, Marge notices the tan Ciera parked by the lakeside cabin. Without waiting for backup, Marge approaches. The sound of a wood chipper is heard from the distance. By the time Marge gets close enough to see who is operating the power tool, we too see a gruesome sight. Gaear is feeding the remains of his accomplice into the loud machine a rather large area in front of which is covered with blood. When Gaear realizes she is there with a gun held on him, he throws a piece of log at her and starts running. Marge fires a warning shot then shoots him in the leg.

Marge's observations and questions as they sit in her prowler with Gaear in the back seat, handcuffed and behind the bars separating the back seat from the front, are a telling commentary on the "theme" of the movie as a whole. She realizes that the body in the cabin was Mrs. Lundegaard and that the remains fed into the wood chipper were the body parts of Gaear's accomplice. And, of course, the three dead in Brainerd. "And for what?" she asks. "For a little bit of money. There is more to life than money, you know," she tells the ever-taciturn Gaear, who looks at her with a blank expression on his face. "I just don't understand," says Marge in the end. The final two scenes complete the series of contrasts the movie has been presenting us with since the beginning. We see Jerry's arrest in a remote motel in North Dakota and we see Marge and Norm in bed. It appears that Norm's design for a postage stamp has been accepted and will be a three-cent stamp. Marge is happy for and proud of him. And consoles him over the mere three-cent stamp by pointing out to him that people need the little stamps when the post office raises the rates and they find themselves stuck with the old ones. "I love you Margie," says Norm. "I love you Norm," says Margie. Then both repeat the words "two more months," the time remaining in Marge's pregnancy, as the movie fades out.

In conclusion let me return to the biblical quote with which I started: "For the love of money is the root of all evil." The passage continues with the words: "it is through this craving that some have wandered away from the faith and pierced their hearts with many pangs." I am sure that the movie has not been perhaps deliberately trying to illustrate this very point, but it has certainly done so anyway. And I am not sure why "Fargo" was chosen as the title, but I can't help feeling that perhaps the question "how *far* would people *go* to obtain unearned money?" may have been instrumental in the choice. This question may remind some of a famous short story by Tolstoy in which a man is promised as much land as he can encircle by running. His greed makes him run and run and run until he drops down dead.

Since throughout the movie we have been presented with contrasts between the wages of greed and the unassuming and unpretentious rewards of love, perhaps I should end with a few quotations from another of St. Paul's Epistles (1 Corinthians 13:4-7): "Love is patient and kind; love is not jealous or boastful; it is not arrogant or rude. Love does not insist on its own way; it is not irritable or resentful; it does not rejoice at wrong, but rejoices in the right. Love bears all things, believes all things, hopes all things, endures all things."

About the Author

A semi-retired professor of literature, Steven C. Scheer earned a Ph.D. from The Johns Hopkins University in 1974. He taught for just about 30 years in a liberal arts college as well as in several universities. He wrote many essays and a couple of books (the last is *Pious Impostures and Unproven Words*, a study of the works of such classic American writers as Hawthorne, Melville, and Mark Twain). He was always popular with his students, partly because of his irrepressible enthusiasm and partly because he invented such "fun" assignments (about which he also published an essay) as "The Fictitious Term Paper."

When the liberal arts college for which he taught for decades went out of business, Steven C. Scheer decided on a new career. When he was young he really wanted to be a writer, so now at the age of 60 he is starting all over again. *Hollywood Values* is his first offering as a full-time writer. It is an act of love, as it were, based on a lifelong appreciation of good movies, along with plays and novels and poems, of course. He is already at work on his next book (*Love & Death & Sex & Marriage*), for which the groundwork has been laid years ago in his teaching of certain courses that touch upon the development of romantic love in Europe and America. Wish him luck.

Printed in the United States
4260